Sweet Footed African:
James Jibraeel Alhaji

As told to
Francis B. Nyamnjoh

Langaa Research & Publishing CIG
Mankon, Bamenda

Publisher:
Langaa RPCIG

Langaa Research & Publishing Common Initiative Group
P.O. Box 902 Mankon
Bamenda
North West Region
Cameroon
Langaagrp@gmail.com
www.langaa-rpcig.net

Distributed in and outside N. America by African Books Collective
orders@africanbookscollective.com
www.africanbookcollective.com

ISBN: 9956-792-75-6

©James Jibraeel Alhaji & Francis B. Nyamnjoh 2015

DISCLAIMER
All views expressed in this publication are those of the author and do not necessarily reflect the views of Langaa RPCIG.

Table of Contents

Chapter 1: Hero Days in Primary School..................…..1

Chapter 2: Secondary School Life...........................…..21

Chapter 3: My First Love........................…............…..37

Chapter 4: Life in high school.....................…..........…..55

Chapter 5: My Days at the University of Yaoundé..........67

Chapter 6: Saudi Arabia Beckons.............................…..77

Chapter 7: South Africa Imagined and Pursued……....…..115

Chapter 8: Graced by South Africa...........................…..159

Chapter 9: My Wife Never Understood the Business..187

Chapter 10: Life as an Immigrant Businessman in South Africa...…......…..205

Chapter 11: My Mother Was a Very Good Friend…..…..... 237

Chapter 1

Hero Days in Primary School

I am a Cameroonian immigrant. I live in Cape Town. I have been in South Africa for almost 20 years. When some years ago there were outbreaks of violence here and there in South Africa against black immigrants from other African countries – those usually referred in most unflattering terms as *makwerekwere* –, many journalists, along with academics and students came knocking to interview me. The questions they asked, however deep they tried to be, always left me thirsty and hungry, wishing they had gone this way or that way, explored this or that theme, dug deep, or followed a particular line of enquiry to a crescendo that did not always serve the purpose of overly simplifying the issues or my situation. They would stop only when I was warming up to a serious conversation, warming up with surging questions of my own. I detested the tendency to see us, a priori, as a problem and the resistance, even by those who should know better, to see the extent to which we were more of a solution than an encumbrance.

Sometimes I followed the accounts of their interviews with me and other immigrants on radio or as articles in newspapers and on blogs. Although I have never read the more scholarly accounts in theses and dissertations written by students, or in books and journal articles by interested academics posing as migration experts, I have often wondered why very few of them have ever treated me as if I had a life prior to my arrival in South Africa. Few want to know how I came to be here. They imagine and impose a reason on me for coming to this country, often in contradiction to what I tell them if they bother to ask. And, even as they are interested in my life in South Africa, their questions often leave me perplexed as to why they frame things in such terms as not to do justice to the fullness of my life and experiences as an immigrant in their beloved country. Many suppose that I am here to stay, that I would do everything to remain in South Africa, and that the country I come from is not worthy of modern human life, which is why – they suppose rather than ask me – I am running away, and have taken refuge – illegally, they love to insist – in South Africa, in my desperate quest for greener pastures. Nothing I say, or wish I could say in the interest of nuance, seems to matter in the face of such arrogant and admittedly, it must be said, ignorant accounts.

My frustrations with what I read and hear have pushed me to the conclusion that South Africans would perhaps understand and relate with much more accommodation if they were to get to know us, *amakwerekwere*, in our wholeness as human beings – as people composed of flesh and blood, people shaped and humbled by the highs and lows, whims and caprices of human existence – and not simply as statistics of inconvenience or as odd strings of phrases, often quoted out of context, to illustrate news stories by journalists in a hurry to meet deadlines. Sometimes the impression is strong in me, very strong indeed, that some are reluctant to allow such a thing as reality to stand in the way of a good story. Sensationalism craved to the detriment of the complex messiness and intricate interconnections of the everyday lives of South Africans and *amakwerekwere* in urban South Africa.

As I say, I haven't read anything academic, not being one myself, so I don't know how better or worse off they are from journalists, in how they, in their scholarliness, capture our lives and predicaments as black African immigrants in South Africa. Whether or not they are less obsessed with documenting how best the South African state and people could control the influx of undesired immigrants flocking in like locusts to dissipate their industrialised economy – the leading economy in Africa, as they often stress, refusing as much as possible to give giant competitors like Nigeria (poised to overtake South Africa to become the leading economy in Africa in a few years) the slimmest of chances –, spread dangerous diseases and enshrine crime, chaos and foreboding, such academic accounts, like their counterparts furnished by journalists and mouthpieces of the various shades of the Rainbow, stand to benefit from more profound knowledge of *amakwerekwere* as flesh and blood steeped in histories, both personal and collective. If the intention and determination of the chroniclers of daily life in South Africa are to control *amakwerekwere* – real or imagined – what can a fly like me do to stop an almighty bulldozer elephant pregnant with zeal? But I believe that by contributing this very modest and personal account in as detailed a manner as possible, the elephants of South Africa are likely to find substance in it to make informed decisions vis-à-vis this strange species of flies they call *amakwerekwere*.

Before I proceed, I have one confession to make. I am not a good storyteller. I have grown up reading and appreciating the stories of others, stories told in the moving colourfulness of language masterfully harnessed. That I could never imitate, however much I try, and God knows I have tried. So my dear reader – whoever you are – please bear with me. I plead for compassion, understanding and forgiveness as I dabble into a field in which I command little expertise. I have been tempted many times to simply let an accomplished storyteller takeover my story and render my existence fictitious, in the manner of the hunter telling the story of the hunt. Each time tempted, each time I have resisted. It is my conviction that my story is best told by me in person – however defective my style and however appalling the sound of my voice – than left to perfect strangers who, however sympathetic and engaging vis-à-vis my predicament, can at best only reduce my experiences to theirs in the manner translators and interpreters – however accomplished – are known to reduce the words of foreign tongues they do not quite master. With this confession behind me, let's begin from the very beginning: where I was born and grew up, the relationships that have made me, the nimbleness of being that has characterised me, and how I came to find myself in South Africa, where I have lived and worked for nearly 20 years.

* * *

This is the story of my life. The funniest thing with me is that I don't know when I was born. I don't know my date of birth. The reason for this is that when I was born there was no one to record it. The only person who could have taken note of the time and place: my uncle, D. O, did, but he then lost it again. D.O is my mother's brother, the *chopchair*, as we call clan heads in my region of Cameroon. He is very active in Southern Cameroon circles. He was the one eye that we had in the family at the time. He wrote my birth details down, but he subsequently lost the book in which they were kept. I have made so many failed attempts to find my date of birth. My parents could remember that I was born around 1963, but not the month nor the day I was born on. From what they could tell me, I know I was born in the rainy season. There was a lead when I found out that a Pastor in the village at the time had apparently written it down as well. Again, I don't know what happened, but he, too, couldn't find the record. Before I knew that I was certainly born around 1963, I had already chosen 5th March 1965 when I had to establish an official birth certificate. I chose that date for my birth certificate even before I realized

I was born during the rains. It turned out that when I got the description, it fitted 1963. On my birth certificate, I am at least two years younger than I actually am.

I was born in the Ngali Quarter in the then Pinyin Village (now Pinyin Clan), Mezam Division of the then North West Province of Cameroon. My parents moved from their big compound in Ngali when I was still very young. I can't remember the details of that move, but I do know that we moved to a place called Payak. Today we call it Payak City, but in those days it was a vast farmland. Ours was one of the families that lived and farmed there. So, I basically grew up on a farm.

I remember my childhood in Payak, particularly when I was going to primary school. We had to walk some seven or eight kilometres to school in Kwindegli, another quarter of Pinyin. At the time it was very difficult to find a primary school. We had to walk long distances to get to one. It's not like today where schools are everywhere. We even have one right in Payak these days.

It was fun going to primary school. I had a great group of friends and acquaintances at that school. One particular friend is of blessed memory now. We called him Njzenge. But some pupils nicknamed him Njzenge fufu, which means, "a bundle of fufu", because he came late to school repeatedly. According to some of the pupils, Njzenge came late to school because every morning when he got up he wanted to eat a big bundle of fufu before he left. That was not true, but it didn't stop the pupils from claiming and believing it was.

Njzenge was my friend. We were always late to school together, because we lived so close together. So, when they called him "Njzenge fufu", they called me "Nkhaa atsu", which means "a bundle of atsu". According to them, I used to eat atsu early in the morning before I came to school. We were really good friends, Njzenge and I, but he is no more.

I had other friends. But, they were bullies as well. I remember one in particular: his name was Ntong. He was a few classes ahead of us; he used to bully us a lot. Later on in life Ntong abandoned school to become a thief, stealing cows from Pinyin, Bali and other neighbouring villages as a way of life. It is said that when he got hungry, he would butcher a big cow and eat it all up, roasting and cooking it in the hills. When we were at school, Ntong used to arrive on a horse. His father had a lot of cattle, which he used to teach Ntong to herd on horseback. This boy was someone who always got what he wanted. A grave example being that he used to force girls onto his horse, before riding off and raping them.

Besides Ntong, I had a classmate who was also a bully. He was a smallish guy, but everyone knew him to be someone who could beat up anyone, even if they were a giant. We called him Mento. In those days, we took our own food to school to eat during the lunch break. Mento, however, would never bring food. Instead, he took mine. He would take whatever he wanted. He used to beat me up. I was bigger than him but he beat me up anyway. The word around school was that he was so powerful that he could even beat up 10 people at once. So, anytime he approached me for food, I just gave it to him; anytime he wanted anything, in fact, sometimes even my pencils, my books, I had no choice but to yield. On one occasion my school books went missing because Mento had taken them.

After school, we used to leave in a group. I recall one day when Ntong, the bully on horseback, stopped us all from going in our direction. There were quite a number of us, but he stopped us all. At the same time, as usual, Mento was also harassing us. I don't know what happened, but it transpired that the bully on horseback wanted to witness a fight. He said he wanted a fight and needed to choose who would fight whom. Unfortunately, he chose me to fight Mento. He called it a fighting competition. There was no way that anyone could ever back down from a fight once Ntong had declared such a thing. You did what he told you to do.

This turned out to be a bad day for me. I gathered all the courage I could, however. I thought about the bullying – the way Mento had been treating us in school, taking my food and whatever –, and decided this would be the opportunity for me to show this guy what I was made of, to show him that he was no better than me. I still don't know where my courage came from, but I launched into a fight with blind fury. Before I knew it, I had him well beaten. As I would learn from others who sang my praises thenceforth, the beating I gave him was so much so that he did not come to school for a couple of days out of anger at being humiliated. I had won the contest. Ntong wanted to watch a fight. I had given Mento a fight through which I had won my liberty from Mento. From that day on Mento never bothered me again. Actually he made sure we became friends. Mento, like Njzenge, is now no more.

Two camps emerged in school after that day: those who bullied and those who protected those who were bullied. I became the good guy. I never wanted people to be molested by the bullies. Anytime Mento or anyone else was molesting someone and saw me they would stop. Mento no longer dared to take anyone's food in my presence. Pencils and books survived as well. This must have been a delight to many parents who, in turn, did not have to go to the market every now and again to shop for items for their children who reported them missing.

I also remember a particular incident from my time in class seven. In school we had soccer teams. There was team A and team B, and sometimes we even used to have class teams. I don't know now whether it was team A or team B, but I used to be the goal keeper for one of the school teams. In those days Cameroon used to have popular local politicians. One such man was called Honourable Sham Muuffoo. He was known to splash spittle when he spoke, like a machine gun on a shooting spree. Because of the amount of spittle that corrupted his speech, his name had been corrupted to Sham Muufoo. He was a parliamentarian. I can't be exact about the period, but it was after reunification of the English and French speaking Cameroons, around 1974.

If you were a parliamentarian in those days, you were a highly respected person. Honourable Sham Muufoo, as I came to realize, had not been to school. He was illiterate. Yet he was a parliamentarian. Hilarious stories of his unusual exploits circulated like fake currency in a country of failed promises. He planned a visit to Pinyin, and one of his stops was my school, P.S Kwindegli. The soccer team were required to prepare for a match to entertain him. Motor cars were pretty rare in our part of the country and even rarer where our school was situated, so it was rather odd to see a car driving towards the school. It was a big thing for most of us to see and touch the Honourable Sham Muufoo's car – one of those olden day Land Rovers. We shouted "Nana… Nana", because his car reminded us of the only other car we saw once in a blue moon – a bush taxi whose driver went by the nickname of "Nana-man no di know". Nana's was the only car that used to come to Pinyin. People had different stories about that car. They made different songs about Nana; songs they would sing whenever they heard the sound of the car approaching from beyond the distant hills. Nana's Land Rover was a transport vehicle that would ferry people from Pinyin to Santa, and the lands beyond.

So, you can imagine our excitement when the big man, who owned his own car, made his visit. He was obviously more important than Nana whose car was public, that is, available to everyone who could afford the fare. Honourable Sham Muufoo was bigger than Nana, too. Not only was he a parliamentarian, his car was clean of dust and unavailable, and unaffordable, to the public – not even those who had money to pay for a ride could hire it for use. He was the first unquestionable big man to visit us, so we had to prepare very well to receive him.

Honourable Sham Muufoo arrived in his Land Rover. We had a football match to welcome him, team A and team B. He stood to watch the match. Then something happened. While I was a very good goal keeper at the time, there was a particular striker on the opposing side who was determined to score. He kicked the ball and I dived full length. I had never dived like that before. It was a risky dive even for a good goal keeper ready to throw caution to the wind. Why did I dive the way I dived? Because I wanted the Honourable Sham Muufoo to recognize me. I wanted to do whatever was necessary to get recognition.

The problem was that when I dived I fell on my arm and couldn't get up again. I stayed there, lying on the roughness of our bald pitch. I had injured myself. I was carried off the field of play. While our school was not equipped with any first aid, in this instance, it seemed not to matter so much as we all watched The Honourable Sham Muufoo go to his car and bring out a first aid box. That man was organized! I don't know what they rubbed on my arm, but they bandaged it, and used some of the bandage to support the arm around my neck. I was in so much pain, but, being attended to by the Honourable Sham Muufoo, it didn't take too much effort to ignore. He was like an idol after all.

When the Honourable Sham Muufoo was coming the headmaster announced the visit to all the pupils of the school.

He asked each and every pupil to bring something: either a bucket of beans, a bucket of Irish potatoes, cabbages, onions, or whatever. That day, the whole school brought buckets of food. There was no way that the Big man was going to take all of that food in his Land Rover. The teachers profited from it. They helped themselves to all the buckets that the Big man's car couldn't pocket.

It wasn't the first time that the teachers were taking advantage of our parents' harvest. Often, when they were hungry or had to punish us for one misdeed or another, they would ask us to bring bags of potatoes or whatever foodstuff our parents could afford to part with. These teachers never used to buy food and hardly used to farm. Even when they farmed, it was the pupils who did their farming for them. They used to live a good life – life without effort. All they needed to get things done was to punish pupils for one failure or another. Manual labour yielded more tangible results for them than corporal punishment.

One headmaster stands out in my mind from my primary school days. Incidentally, he was called Mr Mofo, he was from Baforchu. I don't know whether or not he was related to the Honourable Big man, Sham Muufoo. But he was nicknamed "Nkepone". He was strict. In those days, to be honest, being headmaster was synonymous to being strict. In the case of Nkepone however, he actually over did it. Maybe it was wickedness, I don't know. There was a gathering of Presbyterian schools that involved activities like sports. The incident I remember concerned a female pupil. The girl was playing handball and the other team scored against us. It happened that they scored through her wing. After the game, that headmaster gave this girl a slap so powerful that she fell, fainted and later died.

This headmaster had a little girl, his sister, staying with him.

She was also the sister of my friend and classmate. At the end of one term, I don't know whether it was first, second or third, I was chosen as one of several pupils to carry food to Baforchu, the home village of our headmaster. It was part of the food they used to ask kids to bring to school. We did not go to Baforchu by car; you had to trek, and the distance was far from short. Baforchu was very far away, and the roads were not good. I had to carry a bag of potatoes and trek all the way to Baforchu. I can't estimate how many kilometres, but it was long. We started very early in the morning and got to Baforchu at midnight. The journey was tough. Even when we were going downhill, rolling the bag of potatoes downhill was out of the question. Tempted though we were, we knew the fate that awaited us should the bag appear scratched by the time we delivered it to the headmaster's compound in Baforchu. It was quite an experience. We got there at midnight. Bih, the headmaster's little sister, classmate and friend of mine, was among us. We gave the food. They didn't ask us to eat. They didn't give us food. They didn't give us a place to sleep. We had to trek that same night to the next village, Allah Tening, further from Pinyin, where one of the boys came from, to eat and sleep, exhausted as we were. Trekking as hard as we were able to, we only got to that village around 5 am. His parents gave us food. We ate, slept, and then we stayed there the whole day, before starting started off the following day again to go back via Baforchu to Pinyin. It was easier going back since we weren't carry anything.

Bih, the little sister of this headmaster, died after only two years in college. Anyone who ever lived with that headmaster died – the wife died, the kids died. He was left alone; and while he is still alive, even today he is alone.. I saw him in Abakwa one time that I was going home. It appeared that he recognized me. I met him on the Commercial Avenue. I looked at him, he looked at me. He is not the kind of person you want to talk to. So, I just passed him and went on my way. Wickedness doesn't pay. Unlike other people that you meet from your past and you are keen to share memories and catch up on various fronts, this was the sort of man to avoid at all costs. It was rumoured that he used to frequent the company of the devil much too often for anyone's good.

The Honourable Sham Muufoo would probably have had room for more buckets of food had it not been for his decision to carry me home in his Land Rover that day of my injury. My quarter was along the way. He dropped me off when he got there and continued his journey. He gave me a few sweets, three or four sweets, something we didn't eat every day in the village, and I was so happy. I was the hero of the school that day. I had entered a motor car for the first time; one driven by a man of Sham Muufoo's stature. I could not feel any more pain at all as I was seated on the soft seats of The Honourable's Land Rover. I sat in the front seat too, next to the driver; I made sure I waved at everyone along the way. The Honourable dropped me off at the junction to Payak and gave me a few "bonbons" -a kind of sweet- to soothe my pain. This was the happiest day of my life thus far. The events of the day even meant that I missed writing my Common Entrance Examination to qualify for secondary school owing to the injured shoulder that kept me out of school for so long.

I had made history. Everyone was jealous of me in school even though I was in pain. And because of that incident I didn't write. It was my right arm that I had injured playing football – the arm I had learnt to write with – and I couldn't handle the pen with my left hand. So I missed out on the Common Entrance Examination, and with it, the opportunity to go to a government secondary school or to one of the top Christian Mission secondary schools in Abakwa city.

I was a sharp pupil. I wasn't going to fail if I wrote, but having not written, I was reluctant to repeat Class Seven, in order just to write the following year. I wrote and passed the First School Leaving Certificate Examination, later that year. With that I could only qualify for a private school – generally perceived of as lower quality –, so I sought and obtained admission into the City College of Commerce (CCC), Abakwa.

Primary school was, generally speaking, fun. Every day I went to school with mischief and was ever enriched by the mischief of the other school kids. We had fun stealing; we used to go and steal avocado from farms nearby, then we would dig the ground and put them inside to ripen quickly. During the lunch break we used to go and dig them out and eat them. We used to harvest bananas from farms, too. This was without permission, but they would keep us going to school. We played little pranks on one another. We cried every now and again because this or that pupil tried to bully us or take more than their fair share of this or that, but in general, it was quite a life – primary school.

Normally my parents were unhappy about issues like the injury of the arm, and the going off to Baforchu! My father banned me from playing soccer after the incident. He didn't want to see a ball because of that incident. I remember a time when I was already in secondary school. I was staying in the dormitory, when my father came to visit one Saturday and found me playing football. We were on the field practicing and he came into the school without me knowing. He saw me playing football. He turned and went back taking everything that he had brought to give me with him. He used to bring me garri – every student's greatest delight of a snack in those days –, all sort of things, and he also gave me money. But, he left and never came back. That is how pissed off he was with me and football.

After that incident, although I liked soccer a lot, I stopped. My parents were strict as well. But then, kids are kids; behind your back, they do what you don't want them to do. Here is another incident I recall.. My father used to go to Nigeria and buy gun powder and matches for sale in Pinyin and Abakwa. He used to go to Nigeria through Nkambe. Once my father was caught with gun powder. At the time it was contraband so he was sentenced to prison. I've forgotten how many years he was there for now but it was quite a while. I was still in primary school then. He was there for at least two years. When he was in prison there was a time when I was driven away from school because of the school fees I owed. The fees were 300 francs. I went to my uncle, my father's step brother. He did not live far from us. He was literally on the next compound to us. With my father either away on long business trips or in prison, this uncle became a kind of surrogate father to me. At least, so it was expected of him. He did not have 300 francs for my fees however.

So, I decided to go to my other uncle some kilometres away from us. He was the only one of my paternal uncles who went to school and was employed by the government. He knew the importance of education. He was the government officer in charge of cleanliness for Pinyin and other neighbouring villages. I went to him and told him that I was driven away from school because of a situation with my owing fees, 300 francs. This uncle refused to give me that money. I would say he refused because he didn't even give me 50 francs nor did he ask me to come back on a later date. Things that people do to you when you're a small stick; I remember this incident as if it occurred yesterday. This is someone working for the government and staying in his own compound. He knew what school was, yet he refused to give me the money. He came up with an excuse. As a consequence, I didn't go to school for quite a while. My mother had to sell the foodstuff she farmed to raise the money for me to go back to school. We raised the money together and I went back to school. This is an incident that refuses to leave my mind. Anytime I see my uncle, no matter what he does, I see him saying: "I don't have 300 francs." I see him saying exactly that, so much so that I don't feel anything for him. It's like he's not even my uncle. What I will do for my other uncles I will not want to do for him. That's the way I feel.

My mother used to suffer a lot. I was very troublesome when I was three or four years old. Being the first and only child at the time, my mother used to carry me on her back as she went about her chores. Later, when my sister was born, my mother's junior brother, Ni, used to take care of us. He left us when I was virtually grown up, going to primary school and feeling like the big boy I so desperately wanted to pass as. Then Eli, a maternal aunt, came to take care of us. She became like part of the family.

When my father was with us he used to love the avocados on our farm- and there were a lot of avocado trees there. There was a particular avocado tree that bore very good fruits. It tasted good – there was no water inside. My father named that avocado tree "Papa's Pear Tree". What that meant was that even if it drops, you take it to papa, you don't eat it. It belongs to him. There was no talk of harvesting it. That was out of the question! You don't harvest until you're ordered to. One day, my cousin and I were being very adventurous. She actually convinced me that we should go and harvest those pears – 'pears' is the regular way we referred to avocados at home. . Since I was the man I had to climb. She was the woman so she had to gather the pears. I harvested and dropped the pears for her to pick up. We then took them home.

I don't know what we were thinking, I don't know how she

convinced me to even take the avocados home. I was still very young and silly. Unfortunately, my father came back home earlier than we had anticipated. He used to go to distant places – Nigeria, Kumba and Abakwa, to name just a few – buying and selling stuff. After his time in prison he stopped going to Nigeria, and became a cattle trader. He started going to places like Nkambe to buy cattle and would go on to sell them in Abakwa, Kumba and other distant places in the south and coastal regions of our country. He used to travel a lot, so I guess we brought those pears home thinking there would be no danger. But, unfortunately for us, my father came back and was met with those pears. Wow! Imagine the beating! It was after he had been to prison and back. So he had learnt how to punish people thoroughly in prison. He clamped my feet together and transported me to hell with his beating. Today, my knees still bear the scars of that clamping and beating. Anytime I look at my knees, I think about the pear tree with the forbidden fruit.

I told my father this story when I went back home to the village some years ago to complete a house he was building in the compound. He had fallen sick and, so, couldn't complete it. He was really sick. I took him to the hospital. I left him there. While he was being attended to in Mbingo Hospital, I was busy fixing the house. I took down the ceiling and put up a new one, made many structural changes and generally renovated the entire structure. People who saw me working on the house thought my father had died, and rumour spread that I had put him at the mortuary to fix the house before bringing him home. I didn't tell my father that I had come home to renovate his house. He thought I had come to take him to the hospital. I didn't know he needed that kind of attention. I just arrived and met him in sickness, so I took him straight to hospital. . I was shuffling between Mbingo Hospital situated in the distant land of Kom well beyond Abakwa and Pinyin. In the end, I brought him home from the hospital and then left him in Abakwa for a while in order to finish the house. He didn't know what was going on.

I took him home after the house was finished. I organized a dinner for the family. It was a big thing that involved inviting other villagers close and distant. It was like I was giving him his funeral celebration before he had died. I brought him into the compound. Cows were slaughtered. He was so surprised. He became dumbfounded when he entered the compound and looked at his house. He could not recognize it. I took him inside. I had bought lounge chairs, a dinning set, and a central table. He stepped in, looked around, and gave up: this was certainly not his house.

It was a big occasion. A cross-section of Pinyin was there. In my speech, I told my father the story. I showed him my legs. I told him the story of the pear tree, how he had clamped my legs and beaten me until I could see hell beckoning. That notwithstanding, I told him "I still love you, because I know you did it with good intentions". He was my father and always will be. I understood that his treatment was not because he hated me, nor for what I had done. Rather, it was to discipline me, to prepare me for the future and for life away from home. It was very emotional. He was happy that I forgave him.

My father was very strict, and that's probably why in my family we are so disciplined. With the exception of one or two youngsters, we are very disciplined, thanks to that upbringing. So my father was very important in my upbringing. He was a very hard working person, he never wanted to deal with lazy people. My mother was the same. I was the first born to my father, and the first born to my mother as well. Sometimes my mother would go away for a birth or death ceremony in a village nearby, or to visit relations, for one or two weeks, or even more. My father was not around for much of the time, especially when he was trading in Nigeria. I was still in primary school. I fitted well to take care of my younger siblings. My parents could go away and leave the whole house to me while I took care of my junior ones. I used to pound atsu, the famous cocoyam dish with yellow sauce which my region of Cameroon is renowned for. I used to cook for them. I used to go to the farm and farm like a woman. I was brought up that way. That's the kind of life I lived. I was brought up to easily replace my father and my mother. But the junior ones after me didn't go through all that. It is probably why I am so attached to the family. If I see one of my junior ones doing something that I think is not good, it makes me sick. If I can't get them to stop, it makes me very sick. Two of my junior brothers are making me really sick at present. They are not doing what they should be doing, despite all we have done to keep them on the straight and narrow.

One of the brothers keeps imagining himself as a rich man one day – I don't know by what magic given his effortlessness – building a hilltop house and owning a fleet of buses. We all know where his armchair ambition comes from. As we were growing up, there was this man who came from Nigeria, fleeing the Biafra war. The man used to be a driver in Nigeria, driving a bus and when they were repatriating Cameroonians for meddling in a war that did not concern them, he came back home with his own bus. Then he came right to the village and he built his house on a hilltop, far from us, far from everyone. The house was perched on a hilltop like a bird overlooking the rest of the village. Like a witchdoctor charged with protecting the innocent from the harmful exploits of the witches in the village, he could stand in front of his hilltop house and see people miles away. It is this man who inspired my junior brother to start dreaming without effort to buy that hill because it is the best site in that village.

When this man built his house, he paid people to dig the road to that house, a road wide enough for him to drive his bus on. The bus was the only car in the village at that time. If someone was sick, you had to go to this man and plead with him to take the sick person to hospital. If you had to go somewhere, if you had to go to the market in Santa, you had to use that bus. As children, we never knew that man by name. Even today, if you ask around, most people there don't know his name. We used to call him Box 9 in those days. I didn't know why. It wasn't until a recent visit to the village that someone told me why we used to call the man Box 9. It was because his bus was a 9 seater bus. But because the Pinyin man was what he was, the villagers forgot about the 's' and added 'x', and so called him Box 9. This man was a very good storyteller, unlike me. People used to keep his company even when he wasn't driving them anywhere, because he was such a good storyteller. In addition, he had a shortwave transistor radio set that never seemed out of batteries, and that was fond of Nigerian radio stations, which we loved for their good music and the peculiar languages in which they emitted. His only enemy in the village was the raining season. When it rained the roads were very slippery and it was nearly impossible for him to go anywhere with his Box 9. At other times, when the sun was smiling and people were itching to travel, you would find villagers queuing up on the way to his hilltop house; days in advance, they would stand there in order to make reservations to travel.

My primary school days were really eventful and I remember the fun memories more than anything else. I remember that I used to be very hard working as I grew up, having started much earlier than was the norm in the village in my childhood days. From school we used to go to the farm.

Being the first born I had to play the role of a boy and a girl at the same time. I learnt to hoe like a woman, and would follow my mother to the farm, and farm the way a girl child would. As the first in the family, called upon to perform by my father and my mother alike, I mastered the roles of a girl and a boy equally. I grew up with that, so much so that even when I was in secondary and high school, I used to go home to the village and still farm. You could find me pounding atsu and preparing the family meal, things which in other households seemed confined to the girl child. All those things that were meant for ladies I was doing because there was no one else in the house to do it. I was fortunate to have had the upbringing that I had.

Chapter 2

Secondary School Life

Secondary school life was very eventful as well. Being the first born, I could say that I was the first one in the family to go to secondary school. My father loved educating kids. He didn't go to school himself, but he was very much interested in sending his kids to school. His regular trading trips to Nigeria meant that we didn't lack anything we needed for school. He would always go to Nigeria and bring us nice bags, pencils, exercise books and other stuff, even if only for us to lose them subsequently to the bullies. When I finished class seven, I could not go to a government school since I did not write the Common Entrance Examination. At that time they thought government schools were the best, and private schools, especially the non-mission ones, were considered places where the rejects went. When I didn't qualify for government school, my father got me admission into the City College of Commerce (CCC), Abakwa. In those days it was a Pinyin school; it was owned by a Pinyin man. And it was doing well at examinations such as the General Certificate of Education (GCE). Longla Commercial College (LCC) was the other school owned by a Pinyin man. But Longla was not doing so well. CCC was more popular. There was more discipline in CCC. There was more passing of the GCE. CCC was actually the best alternative considering I hadn't qualified to go to government school. The missionary schools were never an option as my father simply could not afford the huge sums of money they expected students to pay as school fees. So to CCC

I went.

When I went to CCC I stayed in my uncle's house in Meta quarter, that was from Form One to Form Three. I was living in Meta quarter with my cousins, Ghama and Vanyam, who were very rough. My uncle gave us two small kitchenette type rooms. We shared both rooms which could only fit two single beds. Yet, my cousins loved bringing home friends who would then live with us for lengthy periods at a time. Ghama is my grandfather's son. My grandfather is actually my father's elder brother because he was like the successor or the clan head- to which I have already referred to: the *chopchair*, in Cameroonian parlance. He used to like me a lot. We were class mates, even though we were at different schools. He liked clothes and shoes the way Satan likes to kill men, as we would say in pidgin English. When he wished to he could go hungry for a month to save up to buy a pair of shoes for himself. We used to call him *Sappeur*. He never wanted cheap things; he wanted expensive things. He was not the sort of person to be caught shopping for okrika. He also liked nightclubbing and adored the company of beautiful women in their prime. If it rained during a party, he would rather be ridiculed for walking barefooted than let himself be persuaded to wear his expensive shoes and walk the muddy meanders of what we call roads in Cameroon. Needless to say, this son of my grandfather's prefers a life well lived to studying.

He used to have so many bad habits and one of them was smoking. One day – I think I was in Form Two or Three at the time – he and my cousin, who believed in smoking, gave me cigarettes and insisted that smoking was good; "It makes you a man," they said, giving me a cigarette to taste. I tried, but it didn't work for me. I ended up coughing. When you are young, you're also childish.

On holiday in the village Ghama and Vanyam offended

me. We were not reasoning in the same direction. Their life was not my life. So when they offended me I went to report it to granddad. They didn't cook. I did all the cooking, and when I cooked, I would save some food for myself to eat later. One day I came back from school to discover that the food I had reserved was gone. They had eaten all the food that I kept. This was the last straw. I had also noticed that they would wear my shirts, without asking for my permission. These things annoyed me so much. I went to report to granddad and I expected them to be punished. I told granddad that they smoked. Granddad used to tell his kids, "Please whatever you do, never smoke a cigarette. It's not good. It's detrimental to your health." I thought because he hated to see people smoking, he would punish these guys for doing it. . So, I went and reported my cousins. He called all of us. We went and sat in the parlour. He told them what I said, and asked if it was true. "Don't lie to me; is it true that you smoke?" They couldn't lie because my grandfather was the kind of person who, if you lied to him, would discover the truth and give you more punishment. So they couldn't lie. They confessed that they used to smoke, but they also added that James smoked as well. I used to be called James at that time. I said, "That's a lie, how can you be lying?" He asked them, "Are you sure of what you're talking about?" They insisted they were telling the truth. The instance that they used to convince granddad that I was a smoker was the day they gave me a cigarette to try. That was when I tried smoking, couldn't stand it and started coughing. I said I remembered, "But I only tasted it. You asked me to taste it, I tasted it and it wasn't good." My granddad turned to me and asked me, "You say you tasted it but you are accusing them of smoking; if it was poison that you tasted would you be here talking to me?" He declared me just as guilty as my cousins.

That incident has meant a lot to me in the future. I became a smoker. To me, it was unfair that my grandfather would let my cousins go unpunished. So I concluded it was OK to smoke. Then, one day I was with the same brother Ghama. It was during holiday in Ngali. We went to the shop and bought a cigarette at night, which we decided to share. Ghama had smoked and so he gave it to me. He was in front of me. I was following from behind. Then suddenly, at one corner, we came face to face with my grandfather. He just appeared. I had the smoking cigarette in my mouth. The cigarette was burning, but fortunately enough it was dark. So what did I do? I could not throw it away. That cigarette was so precious I didn't want to throw it away for two reasons: if I threw the cigarette away, I was going to lose it; secondly, it would be glowing in the dark, and my grandfather would see it anyway. I'd be caught. So I held the cigarette in my hand in a manner that my grandfather couldn't see the light. I don't know how I got out of it but, at the end of the day, my palm was burned in an attempt to hide the cigarette from my grandfather. And the smoke? I had to swallow the smoke, so I started coughing. I had to run to the compound, where I threw away the cigarette. I lost the cigarette that I had burnt my palm with trying to hide from my grandfather.

My grandfather was very strict and sharp. He was not educated, but he did things like help someone with a PhD. I have a cousin, Dr. Zunka. He is a very smart professor of social psychology at the National College for the Training of Marines (NCTM), and well placed at the centre of power in the Capital. In our family it is widely acknowledged that my grandfather would have been more intelligent than Dr. Zunka had he gone to school. That is how sharp he was.

I stayed at Meta Quarters for the first three years of secondary school. I went to the dormitory only in Form Four and Five. The reason my father sent me to the dormitory was because he wanted me to focus on the GCE. He was more interested in me passing the GCE. My cousins used to enjoy life. Ghama would not miss the nightclub, for example. He was in LCC; I was in CCC. We were in the same class. He was so rough. We were staying together in the same house, the same room, the same bed. So, my father decided to send me to the dormitory, in the interest of my studies. I did the last two years in the dormitory.

One of my first, very bitter experiences in college happened when I was still in Form Two. There was a Big – that's how we referred to the more elderly students who elected to protect you as a patron in exchange for your loyalty, service or servitude and food items, sometimes even money. In those days Bigs were really big and elderly, because some came to school rather late in their lives. My Big was one of those old, fatherly-looking types. His name was Bah. He was from my village. But he didn't have much power because he was not a prefect. Real power resided with the school prefects, and you didn't matter as a non-prefect even when you were in Form Five. He belonged to the group of Form Five students we referred to as Floor Members. Their decisions or wishes could easily be ignored or contradicted without much consequence by a prefect. So it happened, in my case, the senior prefect, named Ivo, gave me punishment, from which my Big, though claiming to be friends with the prefect, could not save me. Prefects were like gods in school. Senior prefects were feared more than the principal. I don't know what I did. Maybe I came late to school or something. Ivo punished me by making me mop the grass field, the football field. He also told me to mop the soccer field. So, I did. To do this, you had to put water in a container, put soap inside, take a rag and then mop. It was not synthetic grass. I had to mop the field of real grass.

When I had mopped a portion, he would come and say, "It's not good. Start again." As long as he decreed the field unclean, I had to keep mopping. Repeatedly, I mopped the same portions over and over until he reluctantly allowed me to move onto the next. It took me all day, and still the field wasn't close to being clean, by Ivo's impossible standards. I missed all of the classes that day. Neither the principal, nor the discipline master could say a thing because Ivo was the senior prefect and senior prefects used to have power. They could even beat you with the cane. Prefects as a whole didn't protect us that much. We didn't have bullies as such, but it was all too easy for your trunk or locker to be broken into and your food – garri, avocado, sardines, biscuits or whatever – to be taken.

I had a friend, Robert, whose father had a medicine store in town. Robert and I used to be regular victims of disappearing garri and avocados. One day Robert told me he had had enough: "I am going to bring something for us to punish those guys who always steal our stuff and never own up." He went to town and came back with Phenergan. This, he explained to me, was medicine - the side effects of which caused excessive itching. . He crushed the tablets into powder and mixed it with the garri we had in our trunks. That night we did not even care to lock the trunks again. But, we were taken by surprise, on coming back from preps., that our Bigs, the same people who were supposed to be taking care of us, were the ones who ate our garri and pretended they hadn't. They were going up and down, scratching themselves so much that they got bruises. To Robert and me, it was fun. I used to be called James. At one point one of them got up and confronted us. "Robert and James, what did you put in that garri?" We said, "Which garri? No, we don't have any garri." Then all of them understood we must have done something to the garri. They started chasing us round and round the dormitory, until some of them caught up with us, and had us well beaten. They couldn't prove it and they could not even report us to management. From that day on, they stopped. So, in the end, it was a good thing that Robert did! Some had to go to the hospital; some had to spend money on milk and honey to calm the itches. It was quite fun catching them, and trying to put a stop to all their little pranks .

I was fresh from the village, not at all familiar with life in the city. College, to me, was like a different world. Going to secondary school in those days was quite something. We went through the normal initiation phase into college life – from our time as foxes in Form One to Form Five where we were the big boys of the college, commanding others, if and when the disciplinary authorities allowed us. One thing that stood out for me was the socials. In CCC, they used to have tea time parties. Tea time was when students were invited to enjoy themselves in one of the college halls, with music. I remember one day when there was a social in school that I went to. We could not go inside. We were still too small, and I could not even afford to pay the gate fee. Along with some others, I stood there by the window peeping inside. We saw these big students dancing with girls, holding hands, and doing things. To us these were taboo. We wanted to be like them though. It was a different environment altogether, and I had to fit in, learn how to accept things.

I also wanted to try out what the big boys were doing. My first love experience came, I think, in Form Four. I was still young, and the lady involved actually played a very important role in my future, in my life; even till today. She has shaped my life in a way. I don't know if it is positive or negative, but she shaped my life a lot. She did a lot to me; my adventures later on were influenced by her in so many ways. I am not into lots of relationships. She was the love of my life at the time, and afterwards, and for a very long time. She was from Nso and a

Princess from the royal family of the Nso Clan. I used to go on holiday in the Nso Royal Palace because of her. We were supposed to get married. But, that's another story. I will come back to that later.

Students always want to break rules. When I moved into the dormitory, there was a particular day when we decided to go to the nightclub. It was a Saturday. The popular nightclub in those days was Ideal Park Hotel, just below today's Congress Hall; it used to be the Abakwa Motor Park, around the area popularly known as Swine Quarter. Ideal Park used to reign. On this Saturday night, we, the Big students, decided to go to the night club along with a cross section of us from the dormitory.. We decided to dress our beds up with pillows, some borrowed, as if we were sleeping. Even our slippers were arranged to look as if we were in bed. Of course, we had warned the junior students against saying a word about our whereabouts to anyone. Then we ordered them to sleep, before we went to the night club. It was fun. I still remember the song that was playing that day as we walked into the club. It was *Ring My Bell* by Anita Ward. Much later in life, I would search for that CD. I did eventually find it. I still have it with me today. It is always in my car.

We were dancing and dancing, when all of a sudden, our fun came to an abrupt end. Tom Mboya was the dormitory master and the discipline master for CCC. He was like an old guard headmaster, strict and full of tricks. He had disguised himself and had come into Ideal Park without us knowing. He entered the dancing hall while we were dancing to *Ring My Bell* and he made sure he danced along with us. In a night club, you don't care who is dancing with you if you're enjoying yourself. So, he came and danced with each of us, looking at our faces. We, of course, did not know who he was, because of his disguise. He would leave one group and go and dance with the other group, before, at some point, the news just went round the hall: "Tom Mboya, Tom Mboya!!!", Tom Mboya was a Kenyan politician who was shot dead in Nairobi. We had nicknamed him Tom Mboya probably because of his surname. So it went from lip to lip, "Tom Mboya, Tom Mboya Tom Mboya!!!"

Before we realized it, the hall was dry. But Tom Mboya was faster than us. He went and stood by the gate and said we could not go out. The only way left for us to escape was to jump over the fence at the back of Ideal Park. The place was riddled with swamps! That's where they threw bottles and sharp objects no longer desired. It was terrible, so many of us were injured. Still, we found our way back to the dormitory. We were used to climbing fences. We still had to go into the dormitory through a fence because we didn't pass through the gate of the school. Before coming to Ideal Park, Tom Mboya had already gone to the dormitory, done his inspections and known that we were out. By the time we came back the beds were scattered. Some students, being what they are, while bleeding from the escape, still said , "No, I was not in Ideal Park". Tom Mboya would not ask for proof; he was like a tyrant. He would punish you whether or not you denied being in Ideal Park that night. He didn't care. He had us well beaten. I don't know how many strokes, but it was a hell of a beating. Unlike primary school, where teachers preferred buckets of food, in college corporal punishment was normal. He had us beaten. Then he punished us by making us do various tasks in school. Some students were even expelled.

There was one other incident that stood out at this school. I was made a prefect, a works prefect. I think that was when I was still in Form Five. I was prefect all the way up through school, even in high school. As a works prefect, one of my functions was to supervise the cleaning of classrooms. This fateful day, early in the morning, Tom Mboya was inspecting classrooms to see that they had been cleaned. He met cobwebs. He took one cobweb with his forefinger. "What is this?" he asked. Men!!! The beating this man gave me! It was out of this world, imported straight from hell. He injured my hand and I had to go to the hospital. I was admitted to the hospital for a couple of days because of that. It was a hell of a beating he gave me. I left the dormitory. I decided to leave the school dormitory after I was discharged from hospital.

Tom Mboya was a man with split personalities. When you met him at home with his family and children – as sometimes I did when I accompanied his cousin to his home, his cousin being a childhood friend of mine – he was meek, soft, nice and very human. But in school, he was something else– a monster! I didn't understand him. He's such a nice brother at home, he's such a nice father, and he's a nice person at home. When you met him at home, he would pretend that he did not know that you studied in CCC, but when you met him in school he was a different person altogether. That was the kind of person he was. At home he would buy you a Top to drink, offer you anything he could. You could talk, you could play, and you could make jokes with him. But going to school, when he walked through the gate into the school, he didn't joke, he didn't smile, he compromised nothing. He was unrecognisable. He boiled bitterly with inhuman sentiments and attitudes. That was the kind of person he was.

Later on in life Tom Mboya wanted to marry my cousin. By then, he had left what he was doing and became a Police Inspector. I was in high school then. He was working in the same town where I had gone to do my high schooling. He wanted to marry my cousin, who was a friend of mine in the family. She was like my junior sister, and we shared lots of confidences. She would not get married to anyone without me giving approval. Everyone had accepted – parents accepted, all the other brothers and sisters accepted. Tom Mboya was excited that he was going to get married. And then she came to me, I said, "No. He's going to kill you. I don't want you to marry him!" And, in the end, that was the reason he didn't get married to my cousin. I refused, and my cousin listened. She trusted my judgment.

Back in secondary school, as I became used to the city and its ways, I used to act as a matchmaker between girls and Igbo boys. Igbo boys liked women a lot, especially the boys who used to work in the shops in Abakwa's main market. With Igbo traders, the boys who work under them are apprentices who do not get paid. Instead, they are rewarded at the end of their training with what the Igbo normally refer to as settlement. This means that the patron sets up a little business for the graduating apprentice who then goes off to fend for himself. However, in the course of the training, the young apprentices have to satisfy themselves sexually, especially the older boys among them. Most of the time these boys stay with their patrons or bosses, so they used to have agents in schools who would look for girls for them, and would arrange for them to meet these girls. Most of the time, as well, the agents were the ones who would say what the girls wanted, and any meeting between the Igbo boy and the girl would be left for the dying minute. For those of us who served as agents or go-betweens this was one of our sources of income. We used to call the Igbo boys "Nna'aa". They didn't have money; they stole from their bosses so they could spend easily. When they stole money they wanted to spend it fast, in order not to get caught with the money by their bosses. Sometimes, we deceived them into thinking that we had arranged for girls, only for them to pay us the money and realize there was no girl. I guess that was our own 4.1.9 scam, but it was all in the name of life. It was part of growing up. I remember one day when I had arranged a meeting between a girl and one Igbo boy. I took so much money from this guy, but, at the end of the day, when this guy finally met this girl, after repeated disappointments, the girl never wanted the guy. She wanted me. This same Igbo boy eventually became a close friend of mine. He used to live not so far away from me and where we lived in Metta Quarters. I remember a time when we returned from the village with pork and plantains that my mother had prepared for us to take back to school. One Sunday after church, we sat down to eat the pork and plantains in our little room, when Abasi walked in. He couldn't believe his eyes: Pork meat!!! He screamed "Ghama, Jimmy, chop swine! Chop swine! Swine chop shit, you chop swine? You chop swine." He imitated a pig eating indiscriminately into refuse dumps, physically showing us how the swine eats shit. From that day, I've never tasted pork. I used to eat pork a lot, but ever since he dramatized how dirty the pig is in its habits, I have never warmed to anything with pork in, however immaculately prepared and presented. His mocking face has stayed implanted in my mind. Today, when people see me decline pork, they think it is for religious reasons. I only became Muslim in 1992, but I gave up eating pork in 1982. My father doesn't eat pork either, he never has done. . My mother was the exclusive pork engineer in the family.

In the dormitory there was this night watchman, Naanji, a man from Pinyin. He was an old man. When the cooks left, they always gave him the keys to the kitchen, so he could supervise or watch the cooking corn chaff, which the cooks used to cook overnight. Many students made friends with Naanji. They would bring him beer when they went out, and in exchange, he would dish out buckets of corn chaff for them. Corn chaff was the darling food for students. We used to eat and keep some for later. Some of us relied on the watchman, but other students used to go and steal it. They would break into the kitchen and take the whole pot of corn chaff, and the next day there would be no food for the rest of us. Management said we were the ones who stole the food and so we must go hungry. Their approach was simple: everyone had to pay.

When you go to secondary school, you become a hero in the village. It is particularly interesting to go back home to the village as a college boy. For one thing, you used to wear a pair of shorts but now wear trousers, and you used to go about barefooted but you are now seen around in church, the marketplace and other social gatherings in shoes. It was quite good to feel that way and everyone respected you. Only a few of us went to college out of Pinyin, which had no colleges of its own in those days. Naturally, a college away from the village, especially in a place like Abakwa, was superior to one situated in smaller towns like Santa and Bali. I cherished going back to the village on holidays, because I was guaranteed to stand tall amongst my friends.

In the village at that time there was a lot of money to be made for those who could work. Between Sundays and Market days, when I had the prerogative to show off my trousers, shoes and cityboyness, I used to go and clear farms for people, to make money. That was especially when the holidays coincided with the corn planting season. I would sharpen my cutlass and go out and look for jobs. I could sometimes go out and return with 300 francs or even 500 francs. That was a lot of money at the time. And if it was the right season, we got paid to pick coffee. There were so many ways to make money in the village. It was in those days that I strengthened the habit of fending for myself. I didn't have to wait for my father to buy my books; I could go and make some money myself. I was that kind of person. But, there were so many other students who would lie to their parents and trick them into giving them money. I was brought up to work hard. I was never brought up to be lazy. Holiday or not, in school or out of school, hard work was my anthem.

The one thing that I still remember fully was the fact that while I was in secondary school my father never allowed me to spend my holiday anywhere else other than in the village. He always used to tell us that he would do anything for anyone who first does it for himself. So I grew up with the philosophy that I first have to help myself before being helped. During holidays, I had the habit of going out and looking for jobs like clearing and farming farms. I was used to it. Before I went back to school, first I had to show my father how much money I had raised for myself, so he could add to it. The implication was that if I failed to raise any money of my own, there would be no school fee and no allowance for me that term. Although I liked working, it didn't seem as if I had any choice in the matter. That was the culture I grew up in. I think that has helped me a lot in my life. I've always believed that if I wanted something I must go out and get it. I don't want people to help me if I can help myself.

I remember an incident in secondary school. Then, I stayed in Metta quarter. Sometimes it was tough, when there was no food to eat and hunger would not relent. I had an auntie who had a restaurant situated at the Abakwa Motor Park of yesteryears. It was situated where the Congress Centre is now located, just above the famous Ideal Park Hotel. I used to go and see her when I left school, especially on the days that I was hungry. I would go there to wash dishes and get paid with food, which didn't come automatically. You had to be lucky to be given some rice or whatever leftovers there were. She was a very stingy aunt, that one! If you did not finish the job that she had assigned you, she gave you nothing. In any case, that is how we survived. I would pass there when there was nothing to eat, and would wash dishes, sweep the restaurant and I would get paid in kind – food.

In those days to ride a bicycle was something special. It is comparable to driving a car today, especially in the eyes of a child. Papi was a guy I came to know in Metta quarter. He used to own so many bicycles, which he rented out. When we became friends, every morning we would take his bicycles to his business place, a popular spot on the Commercial Avenue, where he rented them out to children. For 25 francs a child could ride for 10 minutes, and for as much as 50 francs he could ride for 30 minutes. The bicycles were not for hire to go somewhere, but just to take a ride and enjoy it. Along with others, I was charged for taking these bicycles there and bringing them back. This was our own opportunity to ride the bikes, and more importantly, ride them for free. We used to fight to be the first to be assigned a bike. The day that you come late you cursed yourself for coming late. The idea was to get up early in the morning, just to go and ride that bicycle to the place where it was needed for business. We could get up late for school, but never when it concerned taking the bicycles to the Commercial Avenue. That was the life I led then, washing and cleaning up to be paid in kind and in food, and enjoying bicycles which I would otherwise never have done.

That was life in those days. I remember the day I passed my GCE. It was a saddened joy. Unfortunately, most of my friends, with whom I could have celebrated, had failed. Nji was my childhood friend, my very good friend, class mate, dormitory mate and later on roommate at the University of Yaoundé. We were always together. We had six GCE ordinary level papers. At that time in a private commercial school, to have six papers was a great achievement. Those were good results. There was only one other person who had more than us: seven papers. My friend Nji died in a motor accident on the newly constructed Douala Victoria road just before I set out for South Africa. As I left Victoria en route to Cape Town his corpse was being transported from Buea to our home village for burial.

But for this disappointment, it felt good to pass the GCE. It was good to know you were going to high school. It was also shortly after the GCE results were released that I lost money for the first time, a very big amount of money to me at that time. Thrilled with the fact that I had passed the GCE, my dad had given me 10, 000 francs as a present. I used to use a wallet, so I pocketed the wallet with the money. Off I went with Njifor, to enjoy myself. I took some friends and we took taxis to different popular spots and clubs in Abakwa, and then, we headed back home. When we got out at one place, the taxi drove off and I couldn't find my wallet. It was gone, and with it the bulk of the money that my father had given me. Njifor lost some money as well. He had given me his money to keep in my wallet. All of the money went. We could not recognize the taxi because we were drunk. Well, I was not actually drunk but tipsy, kind of. I was not used to drinking alcohol. I had only tasted alcohol for the first time when I was in class seven, when my father got married to his second wife, my step mother. Then they gave me palm wine in a plastic glucose container, known popularly in Pinyin as "awaah nengone". Although I had grown up in a village where it was normal for children to drink palm wine, especially the sweet type which was also often mixed with medicinal herbs, barks and leaves and sometimes honey, I had somehow escaped all of that. So that was the first time I drank palm wine. Then I got drunk and started running around and causing mischief.

Chapter 3

My First Love

Remembering is not like unearthing a pre-packaged truth, but re-membering the various elements that constitute, often without awareness that they are doing so, the building blocks of an individual's truth.

Her name is Judy, The Princess, my Princess and I met her in Form Three, I believe, at CCC. She was the first woman I ever knew in the biblical sense of the word, that is. She was in the same school with me and she was one class behind me. I knew her through my cousin who was her friend. This cousin was like a sister to me.. She used to stay in the same quarter as Judy. I would go and visit my cousin at home as well as in school. We had quite a life together. We were friends for a very long time from that time till after university.

I used to visit Nso, the place where Judy is from. I used to even go there on holiday and she used to visit especially when I was in high school in Nkambe. I remember her first visit to Nkambe. I was staying with my uncle, my Dad's junior brother who is like my father, and his first wife, who is like my mother. I remember her first visit. She came, and I had to introduce her at home as a classmate. Luckily enough she had a cousin who was studying with us in GHS Nkambe. I had to introduce her as a classmate because, even though I was 20 years or more, I was still not expected to have a girlfriend. This thing of boyfriend and girlfriend was like a taboo at home. You couldn't just bring a girl home. It didn't make any difference that I was living far away from Pinyin, as my uncle was behaving the same as my father. So I had to lie. I had to lie that she was a classmate. Eventually, my family came to love Princess a lot. She used to come and cook and help on the farm. She was like part of the family. We were really close.

I don't know how to sort out the memories, but at one point, I had problems with this Princess. When I went to the University of Yaoundé, Princess passed the competitive examination into the nursing school in Abakwa. So she went there to do the laboratory technician course, while I went to the university in faraway Yaoundé. She saw me off at Nkwen motor park. Passing the GCE Advanced Levels and qualifying into university was a big thing for me, and she had to be there, as she had become a big part of my life. While at the nursing school Abakwa, she had a room behind the General Hospital that shared the same premises as the nursing school.

In my first year at university we didn't have cell phones. And, only a privileged few had access to a landline. But, Princess and I used to write letters and send them in the post. We had quite a history together. We had a photo album– a big album that contained a collection of all the photos that we had taken since we met. There was no other person's photo in that album except the two of us. We were planning to get married after both of us had completed our respective qualifications. Between the two of us, we were already living like husband and wife. That's how close we were. But something bad happened.

After my first term at the university, during the Christmas vacation, I went back to Abakwa, full of excitement about seeing Princess. It was while I was in Yaoundé that she had moved into a new room. She had moved to accommodation behind the hospital in order to be closer to where she studied. I knew the area because she had written to tell me about it. I used to go to Abakwa and stay with my uncle, Ni, in Cow Street Nkwen. When I arrived, I left my bags and I took a taxi straight to her place. I went to look for her. Someone directed me. She was not expecting me. I found the place and I went into the room, which was open. But, no one was there. I saw the album in the room. I picked it up and started looking at it to keep myself busy until she came back. I knew she couldn't be far away, as the door was open. As I went through the album, I found a strange photo inside. It was a photo of a guy. Then another photo of the same guy with my Princess, and then another, and another. They were increasingly cosier as the photos followed one another. Further on in the same album, I found two love letters, not from me but from a certain Francis. The one letter was telling her, "You know ever since you left me, I've been lonely. I'm missing you. You must come for the weekend in Mbili ..." I discovered that Judy was going out with someone else. It was such a big shock. I had never known another woman up to that time. I may have flirted now and again, like all youths. I could flirt with one woman or another. But it never came to loving any other woman the way I did Judy. She was the only love that I had. I really loved her and I know that she loved me too. I had discovered something devastating, something that rattled me. I heard someone coming, so I pretended that I had just arrived. A guy walked through the door. He greeted me and I answered. He introduced himself as Francis. I put two and two together. This was the same guy in the letters. The same face in the pictures. His surname definitely sounded Nso. I felt betrayed doubly; Judy had gone back to her home village for her new love. Later, much later, it would transpire that the guy was from *École Normale Supérieure* (ENS) in Mbili, and that he wanted to marry Judy and her parents had accepted him because he was from the same village as their daughter. Her elder sister, the nurse in Mbili, had choreographed the entire match-making.

The guy sat on the bed as though he was the owner of the bed. Then I heard noises from the kitchen behind the house and deduced that Judy was there cooking for him. Suddenly I heard footsteps coming. At first Judy didn't see me as my face was deliberately turned away from the door. When she did finally notice that I was there she dropped the plates and the sound of breaking plates attracted both mine and her new boyfriend's attention. As she dropped the plates chicken and ndole spilt all over the floor.

She didn't want to look at what happened. She ran to me and she behaved as if nothing had happened. She behaved as if that man was not there. I felt bad. She totally neglected him. She wanted to be with me. She ignored the guy until he was forced to react, "You broke the plates with my food but I am hungry, go and get more food. I want to eat." Judy didn't want to go anywhere. It was an awkward situation. I was asking myself, if she loves me that much, how can she do that to me?

Judy didn't move to bring the guy new food and he didn't leave either. He just got frustrated and annoyed that she was not listening to him and just stayed quiet. He didn't leave. I left instead. I had to leave. As for Judy, according to her, the guy should have left for me to stay. She didn't know how much I already knew. She didn't know how much I knew about the guy so she was pretending and I said I had to go. Then she walked me out and encouraged me to go back in. I accepted for the sake of leaving. She didn't even want to talk about the boy. It was like a non-event to her, so I tried to hide my feelings. But she could tell that I was not comfortable. I then left and I never went back. I never went back to her. I knew of course that she was going to come looking for me, so, very early in the morning, I would leave the house and only go back home after dark.

I kept avoiding her. There were some days when she would stay the night in order to try and see me, but, on those occasions, I made sure that I stayed out all night. I kept that up until I went back to Yaoundé. We carried on like that, no communication. She used to write but I didn't reply. It was so hurtful. It really hurt me a lot.

Amazingly, just a day or two after the incident at Judy's place, I met a woman for the first time who I would later marry and divorce. I had a friend, Neil, in Nkambe, who I often spent time with. We were in high school together. We had to go and visit his sister who was staying somewhere in Nkwen. It was there that I met my would-be wife, who is now my ex, the mother of my three kids. It turned out that we were both at the University of Yaoundé and in the same class. But I had not known her then. I had never met her, although she said she knew me. I used to be a flashy and stylish guy with specs, although not as flashy as my cousin, Ghama. I learnt a bit of his style. I was easily noticed. But when we met, she greeted me. She was the first one to greet. I greeted back. Neil knew her because he was used to that area. She was staying in the same area with Neil's sister. When we chatted, she told me we were in the same class in Yaoundé. I was surprised. That's another story. But our first meeting was just a meeting. I met another person immediately after Judy broke my heart, but it was not my intention to meet that person, nor did something develop between us immediately. It just happened that that meeting would grow to become something, and that that something would lead to marriage and subsequently to divorce.

Judy kept trying to communicate with me and meet me, but I kept on ignoring her. For three years at university I successfully ignored her as I single-mindedly sought to fulfil my parent's dream of achievement through my education. In Pinyin, we have this strong belief that when you go to the university and graduate, it means your family has achieved a lot. But then, the feeling of achievement did not actually deliver in my case. I needed more than the feeling of success to survive.

Following university, I struggled like someone who had never been to university – writing *concours* or competitive entrance exams into the public service did not yield much fruit. There was no direct recruitment into anything, and passing such an exam was no guarantee that one was headed for fulfilment of one's ambitions or the great burden of expectations imposed by one's family.

When I graduated with a degree in law from the university, I went back to Abakwa, where I tried to look for a teaching job, which was the most common thing that was there, at that time, for a graduate. I went to my alma mater CCC – City College of Commerce, Mankon, Abakwa. I met the vice principal, a distant relative. There were quite a number of us who arrived at the same time looking for jobs, teaching jobs. I did law and this was a grammar school, but they were teaching law as well in the commercial section of the college. The vice principal was not impressed with the fact that my degree was in law. He preferred to continue with the old person who taught office practice as law. His statement to me was discouraging. He said the college was not looking for lawyers. He instructed me to go to the chambers and practice law. He obviously did not want degree holders as teachers as he had no decent qualification himself.

It was like a mockery to me. But when I had finished fuming and still could not find a teaching job, no matter where I looked, and even after deciding to seek to teach English in French-speaking colleges in Francophone parts of the country, I ended up following the principal's advice. I decided to go back to law. I went to the chambers to start practicing law, but again, at that time, it wasn't easy to get admission into the bar. I was unemployed but attached to Royalty Chambers. I was still pondering if I should practice law. I was with Loyalty Chambers for a while.

Judy had a friend, a very good friend of hers. This friend was working with an insurance company on the same block as the chambers. Grace was her name. So when Grace and I discovered we were working in the same building, she told Judy and in turn she told me Judy's story of the four years that I refused to communicate with her.

I've never heard the story from Judy's point of view. I never knew if I was wrong to ignore her overtures at communication but I was really hurt. So Grace now told me about that guy, Francis. He was apparently forced on Judy by the family because he was from Nso. I was not from Nso. Judy loved me dearly, but the pressure on her was too much. Her parents and her sister in Mbili were clearly in love with having someone who spoke the same language and shared the same likes and dislikes as them marrying their daughter and sister. The sister was the architect of that relationship, she brought them together. Francis was in ENS, and looking for a partner, and there was Judy, going out with someone who was doing a general education degree in law, someone without a future, and above all, someone who was not from Nso. Judy however, broke up with that guy following the incident. She was bent on getting me back. So that's what Grace explained to me. If Judy really did not love him as she and now the story by her friend had tried to show, why did she not let him know upfront? Why had she allowed her photos with him infiltrate the photo album she had led me to believe was special to us only? And why had she given him the license to come and go as it pleased him? What was she doing at his house in Mbili, and why did she think it important to save his love letters away so jealously?

To me and my young lawyer mind, she was guilty as charged. But then, Grace organized a meeting, a blind date, as it would filter through. She invited me to her house saying that she was going to prepare atsu for me. She knew that I loved atsu, so she said I must come and eat atsu at her place. I didn't know I was going to meet Judy. I went there, and Grace opened her room. She said I must go to her room and wait, while she went to the kitchen to get the food ready. I went into the room, and to my greatest surprise, there was Judy. After close to four years without seeing or communicating with one another, there was Judy, looking as beautiful as always. But you could see that she was strained. When she saw me she started crying, begging and threatening to do something bad if I didn't listen to her, because I clearly wanted to leave the room. She locked the door and drummed her mixture of apologies, threats, regrets and anticipations into my ear drums.

Looking back, I can say she really loved me and I loved her back. But by that time, four years later, I had got involved with the woman I met shortly after that incident that derailed our love. Not only was I now involved with this other woman, we actually had a kid, Taanji, and we were planning on getting married. I'd forgotten about Judy, and now, all of a sudden, there we were again, face to face. I didn't know what to do. But the long and short of the story is that we got back together, four years after that incident. Timidly initially, but we became more serious again. I made her understand that I was engaged. I told her exactly what had happened, that I had a kid with another woman, and that I was engaged to marry her. So we got back together timidly, and then we became a bit serious. It turned into a situation I do not like. I didn't like it but that's what happened. To me it was like I was cheating. I felt really bad about it. It became a bit difficult for us to have a fruitful relationship in such circumstances. I really loved her, she loved me and she wanted to be with me, but because I had become involved with someone else, and nothing was going to be the same again, we had to try and reignite the love we once entertained for each other.

So, our second coming ended amicably. I told her it was time we moved on. I encouraged her to settle down with someone, seeing that I had already involved myself with someone else, and had made a child with that person. Eventually, she got married. She had twins by the time I left Cameroon. I've not seen her for a very long time, ever since I left Cameroon. It's a long time now. She taught me a lot of things and she was very instrumental in what I became.

All the same, that coming back together did something in my life. Judy was working at the time. She was now a qualified lab technician posted to work in Foumban. After that meeting, I decided to leave Abakwa and go down to Victoria to practice law with Amnesty Law Chambers. I was a "stageur" or "postulant" as they call a pupil lawyer in Cameroon. Then at one point I wrote the Bar exam and I passed. In Cameroon at the time, passing the Bar exam was like walking straight into money. It was something big. It was a dream come true, passing the Bar exam! I was the fifth in order of merit, out of 60 who passed the exam in the whole country. Before registering to write the exam, I had to go and pay my master's dues at the Bar Council. As the principal of the chambers, my boss owed the council and since I was writing the exams under his chambers, I had to pay his dues to be able to write. So I had to get money from my parents to go and pay for him. The amount was over a hundred thousand francs, a lot of money at that time, and a gift that I am sure he appreciated.

The lawyer's robe in Cameroon at the time was very expensive. They are not even made in Cameroon now. The robe was not something you just went and bought from a shop. You either had to place an order from Britain or you had to go to Nigeria to buy it. The date for swearing in was approaching and I needed a robe. I never had money to buy a robe and I was told that that robe in Nigeria would cost about

70,000 to 75,000 francs. Without cell phones in those days, communicating between towns was very difficult. Even landlines were a luxury which only a few could afford. Fortunately, there was a landline in our Chambers in Victoria, and Judy also had a phone where she worked in Foumban. We used to phone each other every now and again. So faced with this problem of the robe, I called Judy in Foumban and told her that I needed a robe, but didn't have the money to buy one, and asked if she could help. No, no I didn't actually ask her to help. She was this kind and selfless woman. I did not ask her to help. I just told her I passed the exam, and was looking to get a robe, but that I was struggling to put money together to go to Nigeria and get one. She said I had to go to Foumban. So I went to Foumban. She gave me 50,000 francs. In those days that was a lot of money in Cameroon. This was big money, especially coming from her, a mere lab technician, who was category C in the Cameroon civil service payroll. She only had A levels, which meant that she didn't earn much. In fact, she was making less than 50,000 francs a month. To give me a whole month's salary was friendship, indeed, beyond friendship. That's how much esteem Judy had for me.

So I took the money and went back to Victoria. It was not enough however. I had another friend - he is in the US now - Lafah. He actually played a big role in my life. He was a young man of my age but he didn't go to university and he started working at an insurance company after his Advanced Levels. Lafah also helped me out with the robe. He was in Kumba. I went to him with the 50,000 francs Judy had given me, and he added 50,000 francs to make a hundred thousand. Not being sworn in I could not make money at the chambers, even though I worked on a lot of cases the fruits of which went directly to my boss. I couldn't even boast of 10,000 francs of my own. With the money from Judy and Lafah together with the little transport money I had to pay my way from Kumba to Ekok, I set off for Nigeria. This was the first time I was travelling such a long distance alone. I didn't know anything. I just knew that I had to go.

I met Lafah's brother, Greg, in Ekok. He was working with the Department of Forestry at the time. Today he is Executive Director of a very successful International Non-Profit Organisation based in Abakwa. He had a small Volkswagen car in those days, and a driver who carried people from Ekok to Onitsha and back. I was forced to hire it because I had no guide. I don't know how much I paid him exactly, but I think it was something like 15 to 20,000 francs to take me to Onitsha and back. The drive to Onitsha was quite an enjoyable journey.

What I remember about that journey was the Tracy Chapman song – *Talkin' Bout A Revolution* – that the driver played throughout the ride. Today I've got the CD in my car, and I never go anywhere without it. I heard it for the first time in that guy's car. The cassette system was faulty, so it was playing faster than normal, but I did not know that song. So I enjoyed it the way it was played by the defective system. I really enjoyed it and I thought that was how the song was. It happened that it was the only cassette that we had in the car, so we were playing that music over and over. We went and came back with it. When I hear *Talkin' Bout A Revolution* by Tracy Chapman today, I only think about that journey. It was quite an interesting journey.

We went to Onitsha. I remember that I got to Onitsha with about 75,000 francs. We looked for that robe and we could not find it. I was told the only place I could get that robe was Lagos. So I had to go to Lagos. I looked at my finances. Mentus was the driver. He was quite a nice guy. I asked him how much I could pay him to take me to Lagos and back. And he told me the price and I discovered that if I pay this guy, I will not be able to afford the robe in Lagos and still come back to Cameroon. There was no way I was going to get the robe.

So the only other option was to come back to Cameroon. I asked myself how I could go back to Cameroon without the robe, especially as the money I had sweated to raise for the robe was already seriously depleted. I was unlikely to return to Cameroon with more than 50,000 francs left. Then I remembered that people always come to Nigeria, a much bigger economy, and buy things and bring them back to sell in Cameroon. Why not do the same thing, I asked myself. I decided that I was going to buy something to take back to Cameroon for sale. The next question was what? I didn't know. I didn't have an answer to that question. At night an idea struck me. I recalled that Judy had a sister in Nigeria whom she used to visit once in a while, and would return with laboratory reagents she had bought for sale back in Cameroon. Whenever we were together she would talk about how good the business was, and how much profit one could make just buying and selling such things. She was very open, and used to talk about reagents for the testing of syphilis, pregnancy, Hepatitis B and things like that. I didn't know it was going to be useful to me so I didn't want to know more. But now that I urgently needed something, the idea came back to my mind.

So I decided I was going to buy laboratory reagents. The following day I asked the driver to take me to the medicine shops, where I asked to buy reagents for the testing of syphilis, pregnancy, Hepatitis B, and some others I can't remember. It wasn't easy to choose, because each reagent they brought had five to seven different types and specifications, sometimes by country. I was lost. I couldn't phone Judy, so I closed my eyes and made my choice from each lot. I couldn't buy all of them because I didn't have the money, so I took one of each or two of each with my eyes closed and paid for them. I bought reagents for the equivalent of 50,000 francs. Then I returned to Cameroon, went straight to Foumban, met Judy, told her what had happened, and gave her the reagents that I had bought. She could sell them or show me how to sell them to get back some of the money I had lost. She took those reagents and told me most of them, more than 50% of them actually, were the wrong ones.

She said she was going to see what she could do with the right ones. I left her and went back to Victoria. After a week or so, Judy called me in the office and told me I should come up to Foumban. I was worried. I thought she wanted me to pay her, her money back, fearing the reagents I had brought her hadn't fetched much. I discovered afterwards that she never wanted the money back. When I arrived in Foumban, Judy told me "I've sold the ones that were good and I've collected 100,000 francs already for the ones that were good". My eyes lit up. This was a promising area of business. Judy still had close to 50,000 francs to collect from people who had purchased on credit. We had made more than 200% profit from only half of the products I had bought. I decided there and then that I had found a new line of business. I told myself, if there's so much money like this, then why should I stop? She gave me a list of reagents that were required in her hospital in her lab and she gave me back the reagents that were not used in Cameroon, so I could return them on my next visit to Onitsha. She gave me samples of the real ones that they needed. From Foumban, I went straight to Onitsha. I left at night and it took me 3 days, and I was back to Foumban. I didn't sleep in Onitsha. I knew exactly what to do. I arrived in Ekok during the night, took the driver and was in Onitsha by 10 o'clock in the morning. I bought everything. We started driving back. The night of that third day I was in Foumban. I didn't even stop as I passed through Abakwa. I went and gave

Judy those things and went back. My boss didn't know I had even gone out of town, and wouldn't have believed it if I had told him that I had been to Nigeria and back.

Two weeks down the line, Judy called me and said I must come over to Foumban. I went over and she gave me about 300,000 francs from the reagents she had sold already. And she gave me a list of other reagents needed in other hospitals. So I went to Nigeria for the third time with 300,000 francs as capital, bought more reagents and returned. And so, on and on it went. As the saying goes, a disappointment is a blessing in disguise.

The long and short of that business is that I ended up doing it full time. I abandoned legal practice and I started going to Nigeria, buying those things, and going back to Cameroon to sell them. I started doing it myself, and no longer exclusively through Judy. I would go to different hospitals in different regions of the country selling and soliciting interest in the products I bought in Nigeria. The business actually became very successful and in a very short time I bought myself a car. Whatever I gained from that business and whatever I have become as a business man was and is thanks to Judy.

I had not even been working six months when I had enough to buy a car, a Corolla DX- which was very popular at the time. Not just anyone could afford to buy this type of car in those days. So, business was good. The fun thing about my Corolla DX was that I bought it and I started driving the car when I didn't even know how to drive. I bought the car from someone who used to go to Belgium to buy second hand cars and sell them in Cameroon. We finalised the deal at the Commercial Avenue in Abakwa. Then I told the guy to give me the keys. He tried to resist, reminding me that I did not know how to drive, and promising to send a driver to drive the car home for me. I said no, the car is my car, so give me the keys. I remember I was with my Ghama and he too was asking me, but what do you want to do with the car keys? I said I bought the car so I must drive it. I entered the car and I started driving. I had not been to a driving school. I didn't know how to drive but I used to observe drivers, and thought myself observant enough to be able to drive a car without formal training. It was evening by the time we were driving and the roads were not that crowded.

I managed to drive it home. I was staying in Metta quarters. That night we couldn't sleep, me and Ghama, we couldn't sleep. We were driving up and down Metta quarters, going to Nacho and down to Azire and back. We took advantage of the streets not being busy to get used to driving. By dawn, we went back home, packed the car and slept all through the day. At night we started driving around again. Being so business minded, I never wanted to use that car as a private car. I only wanted to use it as a business car. The following night, I actually started doing what they call "clando". I became an unlicensed transporter – taking passengers places in exchange for payment without an official licence to do so. I started transporting people from one place to another, making money with the car. Barely three days into my owning that car I drove it to Santa. The car was often overloaded with passengers. There were normally six or seven passengers that I took in the car. The car was meant only to carry four people in addition to the driver. I was to pay dearly for this overloading, as the engine knocked two times. As with most things in my life, the story of that car is to be told another day.

I left Cameroon incognito. No one knew when I left. No one knew my destination. No one knew where I had gone. I have still not seen nor heard from Judy. I don't know if she knows where I am today, but it wouldn't surprise me if she did. People close to me, who know her, have said that she always asks after me whenever she sees them. I believe we both agreed to move on. Anyway, if either of us really wanted to keep track of the other, it would have been very easy, especially in an increasingly interconnected world like ours, a world where everyone is charged up with ever more modern technologies of detecting and making it impossible for anyone to hide. I know some would imagine that with my relative personal success today, I would have sought to get in touch with her, if not to revive things then to see how she was doing and to thank her for the part she played in my becoming who I am today, without of course reopening that chapter of our lives. In some ways, I've always been planning to do that and I will still do that; but the reason I've not done so yet is that whenever I go back to Cameroon I am never there for a long time. Finding her now would mean going to people and asking, since I don't actually know where she is.

Somehow, I know she is alive and well. The last time I heard about her was over ten years back when she had twins. My brother ran into her. I would not say for sure but I think she is still alive. I would think that she's still alive because if she was not alive, someone who knows someone who knows her or used to be an acquaintance of hers would have brought the news my way, one way or another. But I still want to meet her, probably when I go back home for a longer stay. It is a pity that the only time I made an effort to locate her during a trip to Cameroon, I was looking desperately for her friend Grace, to lead me to her, when, I caught up with Grace's sister who informed me of the sad passing away of Grace. I want to meet Judy, talk to her, and tell her thank you for all she did for me. I also want her to forgive me for all my trespasses, so I could leave her knowing that the harmony we sought in our relationship has graced us at long last. It is never too late to be perfect. Sometimes you lose certain people and it becomes really difficult to get them back. I am not Internet savvy. Maybe if I was internet savvy, I would be able to post messages on Facebook in the hope that Judy might be connected and seek to reconnect. If locating her is the price to pay for joining Facebook, maybe I should explore that option.

When I look back at our relationship, I sometimes feel that I would have been happier if we were together today. She understood me and I understood her and there was true love at one point until the betrayal. I am just thinking that if that incident did not happen, we could have been living happily together today. On the other hand, I want to feel that it wasn't meant to be. This was actually my first true love relationship that I had with a woman. She was the first girl that I actually had had a relationship with, so to speak. I have seen so many childhood love relationships last for a very long time, because they really understand each other and love each other. But I've also seen some fail for one reason or another. I guess I would very much like to be with her today, but, since it was not to be, I've accepted it.

Chapter 4

Life in High School

I completed my secondary school sometime in 1982, at City College of Commerce, Mankon. I went in for seven subjects at the GCE Ordinary Levels and I passed six. The seventh one was a compulsory subject which was mathematics and I did not really write it. At that time City College was one of the best private schools in the then North West Province. Mine was one of the best batches of students ever. In those days, it was not easy for someone to have six subjects in a private school. There were a couple of us who had six papers, and only one student had seven papers. We did well in that batch even though some of my close friends did not make it. And I went on to high school.

I went to Government High School (GHS) Nkambe. The day former President Ahmadou Ahidjo resigned from power – 02 November 1982 – I remember I was in lower sixth. I came to school that day, and I had not heard what happened. I remember everyone talking in little conspiratorial groups, as if plotting something or discussing something that had gone wrong. I could not understand why everyone was so excited. The discipline master himself came to the morning assembly that we always had prior to classes, and confirmed what the radio had announced that morning, that President Ahmadou Ahidjo had given up power. The Prime Minister at the time, Popol, was to be sworn in as the new and second President of Cameroon since independence in 1960. I remember that day vividly, because, with hindsight, it would come to stand for the day the government changed from bad to worse in our country. As I write, the incumbent is still President of Cameroon, over 30 years later, with little but absolute all-round devastation to show for it.

In high school, initially, I was staying with my uncle. He is my father's follower and is still there in Nkambe today. My uncle was like my second father. Even while I was in primary school I used to go to Nkambe on holidays right up to secondary school, and when I got used to the family, I got used to Nkambe. For me, and for most Pinyin people I knew there, Nkambe and the whole Donga and Mantung Division, extending to Misaje, Dumbo and Nyos, was like a second home. There were lots of Pinyin people there. We are a very mobile people. Our feet are always itching to go places. I travelled to all of these places, and had family dotted here and there. But I was staying in Nkambe and studying in GHS Nkambe. Most Pinyin people in the region happened to have invested a lot, and most of them were investing not thinking of going back home. They had farms and lots of houses there, even when they did not have homes and farms back in Pinyin. There were so many of them who never had houses at home but they had more than one house in Nkambe. They had a lot of cattle. It was just like they had come and established themselves in Donga Mantung, and especially in Nkambe. They were economic leaders at the time. When you went into the main market in any major town or village in the region, from Nkambe to Misaje and beyond, the majority of the shops were owned by Pinyin people. It was like a second home to most Pinyin people because they had established themselves so much they never thought of going home again. They considered the region their home. My uncle had made such in roots in the place that he had even been made a *nchinda* – retainer – in the Nkambe Fon's palace. Being the chief or leader of the Pinyin people in the region and having had four sets of twins with the first wife and taken a second wife, my uncle seemed to have earned himself the recognition and esteem of the people of Nkambe, their Fon included.

I remember that marriage fondly. There was a celebration at home. We had a big house. It was quite a big thing. The Fon of Nkambe came for the event. It was time for him to make a speech. The Fon of Nkambe, trying to speak in English, said "Misters Victors is mines sons" … "Misters Victors is verys importants personalities ins Nkambes"… etc. It was not just that he didn't know English. That was the way he spoke. He appended an "s" to every word he used even in his home language. He had more "s" in his vocabulary than anything else. He was such a good friend to my uncle. He actually offered a cow and a couple of goats for that occasion.

Invited as well was a Pinyin man, a pastor of the Presbyterian Church in Tabenkeng. He was supposed to lead us in prayers. I was serving the drinks. This pastor called me, and asked me to serve him the drinks first. I knew at the time that as a pastor he didn't have to drink alcohol. So I went to him with an assortment of soft drinks to make his choice. The pastor looked at me with scorn. There was such disdain in his eyes that I could have run away. He was not like a man of God anymore. He controlled himself, pulled me closer, and said, "Ma pikin, una no get shobasho?" I went and brought him shobasho – Beaufort. When I uncapped it, I could feel my sins forgiven.

The pastor drank, and all the time he would beckon me, bring! He could eat meat, and drink beer. He drank and drank. When it was time for him to pray and deliver the sermon, he asked me to go and get two glasses, one filled with water and the other with Guinness. The sermon was very short, straight to the point. He lifted the two glasses up and said, "Life is like these two glasses, human beings are like these two glasses. If you are a human being and you don't obey God's words, your heart is going to be like this glass" and he showed the Guinness, adding, "black." "But if you're God fearing and you obey God's words your heart is going to be like this one – "white". He paused for a little while, and looked around before concluding: "So it's up to you to choose which life you want to live: black or white." That was the sermon. After that, he prayed. Then I got up to take away the glasses. He gave me the clean glass of water and kept the black one. Then he started drinking his black option for life. I found him strange. It was ironic how he behaved in relation to the ideas of a man of God in which I had been raised. Always, when I meet this pastor, I just think of that incident.

It was my first encounter with him. Presently he's retired. When I went for my father's funeral, he was there and all he wanted, even then, nearly three decades later, when he went for funerals, was to drink shobasho, eat meat and have a lot of food. His nickname in Pinyin today is "Pastor Zdekhe Nnow". Zdekhe Nnow means something like eat and drink. He is pastor eat and drink. He was transferred to Pinyin during his last days before retirement. As if to show how much he loves alcohol, the pastor actually started an off licence bar in a square not far from his church and he involved the whole family in the business. He brought his kids in to serve at the bar. And when you meet those kids today, they have little in them to show that they were brought up by a pastor. Even him, it seems he joined the church more like a business than to render service to God.

That was then. Today things have changed. All the glory is now gone. Many Pinyin people have left Nkambe. If you look at it now, it's only my uncle and two or three others who are there. Hundreds of others have left. I don't know how to explain their departure. The reasons are basically economic. I guess it's because the economy was not doing well. The economy of Donga Mantung went down so much so that they had to go out looking for greener pastures. So many of them left and went to the northern part of the country. Some went to Abakwa, some went back home. My Uncle used to have a lot of cows. He had four herds of cows, which is over 400 cows. I owe what I know about business today to him. During my high school days when I stayed with him, I was involved in many other things than merely being a student. I loved doing business, so I used to help my uncle a lot in the shop he owned at the time. We always went to flea markets in nearby and distant places. I used to like buying and selling. I am so much into business, and my acumen in this connection, I credit to him. I don't see myself working for anyone else. I always like to work for myself. I must have got this approach from those early days and associations in my life with business minded people such as my father and uncle. I don't know if I would survive in a job today. My business activities grew from staying with my uncle. Working with him actually shaped my future as a businessman.

Nkambe has indeed had its highs and lows even for consistently successful people like my uncle – relatively speaking, of course. Today he has barely one herd of cows, no more shops, a couple of houses and plots that have equally drastically been devalued by the slump. Nkambe market used to be vibrant. People used to come from all over and buy from that market. But now there are no shops, the stores are empty, there's nothing there. The demand has gone, and with it, supply. In those days the cattle farming Mbororo were very instrumental to the economy of Donga Mantung. I don't know if it's because they moved. What made the market vibrant in those days were the Mbororo people and their cattle wealth. Either they have moved massively, or they have learnt to shop for themselves from elsewhere, equally mobile as they are.

I went to high school in Nkambe, where I stayed with my uncle for some time before I moved into the dormitory. It was good being in Nkambe during my two years of high school. I made lots of friends, some of whom are still friends to date. The one thing that stands out from my high school days is my encounter with the discipline master of Government High School, Nkambe.

I've always been a prefect at all the schools that I went to. In Nkambe, I was voted the works prefect. Then I was staying in the dormitory, which meant that I had to supervise all cleaning. And if there was punishment, I was the one to give and supervise the punishment. I also knew that I was first of all a student, before being a prefect, and that my studies came first. But there was this discipline master who never knew that. All he knew was that if you're a prefect, you should just be a prefect and not be a student. He saw me as a prefect and nothing more. He had a name but I'll like to remember him as The Devil, as he was popularly referred to in student circles. I have forgotten his family name. With people like him, family names don't matter, shouldn't matter.

There was this incident. I was in school, in class. I remember it was a literature class. I think it was towards exams. It was a very important class. The Devil came and called me out, and said I had failed to supervise some work in school. I refused to go. I told him I was attending lectures and this was a very important class to attend. I told him I really had to attend these classes. And, that I would supervise work later. It was the first time a student had stood up to him and told him, I am not going to do what you say. He was that kind of a tyrant. It was a big thing to him. That's where our problems started. He said I was disobeying him. He said I must go and supervise the work. From then on, we were like cat and mouse; we never saw eye-to-eye anymore. He displayed a lot of animosity. He would take the least opportunity to punish me, to make my life miserable. At one point, it was too much, and I even thought of leaving the dormitory to go back and live with my uncle once more, just to free myself from this overbearing man of discipline.

He used to live next to the school. I don't think he ever wanted me to pass the GCE. I was in upper sixth then and everyone in school knew that if there was one student who was going to pass in the A3 series it would be me. I took my studies very seriously and the subjects I did I did with a lot of passion. When I refused to be subjected to his whims and caprice, he engineered my suspension from school. As a discipline master, he could do whatever he liked. In many regards, he was even more powerful than the principal of the school. He suspended me from school for a few weeks. I couldn't attend classes. He reported me to the disciplinary committee and that is where I got him. The disciplinary committee, 'discom', as it was popularly known among us students, comprised among others the Divisional Officer of Donga Mantung, and the chief of Gendarmerie who, incidentally, would become my good friend following the incident. All those big shots in Nkambe were part of the discom.

I went to the discom and they asked me, why have I been disobeying the authority of the disciplinary master of the school? Why have I not been executing my duties as a prefect? I can't remember exactly what I said. But I went to the front of the disciplinary committee, and in a nutshell, told them exactly what I thought the responsibilities of a prefect were, vis-à-vis those of a student. I told them that I was first a student before being a prefect. I didn't come to the school to be a prefect, rather I came to study. So if being a prefect meant not being a student, then I didn't want to be a prefect, because what the discipline master was doing was tantamount to not wanting me to study. He wanted me to be a prefect and nothing more. We argued, The Devil and I. The disciplinary committee members weighed my word against his. I won their sympathy. They ruled in my favour. It was unheard of in the history of that school that the discipline master would ever take someone to discom and the ruling would be against the master of discipline.

That is where our problems escalated. Like a witch, he told me, "You will see," following the disciplinary committee when I was reinstated and my suspension annulled. I was told to work hard and study hard by the committee. They did everything that was against the way he wanted me to do things. So the animosity escalated. I went back to the dormitory. We were getting closer to the GCE exams. As students, we were used to going for preps in the evening, and studying right into the night, sometimes. One night I carried my books and was going to study, when I met the bitter disciplinary master. He told me, "you're going to study, you're going to read. You want to pass the GCE? You think you will pass the GCE? Not when I am alive. You will not pass."

Seriously! That is what The Devil told me! And I failed the GCE. I failed the GCE and the school and all my teachers went on strike. It was not possible that I could fail the GCE but I had failed the GCE. Quite frankly, I never used to believe in black magic. But that incident made me believe that black magic works, because I failed the GCE. I don't know if it was black magic or simply a matter of him, who also incidentally supervised the GCE writing in the school had done everything to ensure that I did not pass. Maybe after I had written and submitted my papers, he went behind everyone's back and took out some of my papers, making sure that I had failed even before the exams were marked. He might simply have withdrawn some of the booklets on which I wrote, or torn out some of my answer sheets, to give the impression that I didn't answer some questions or that my scripts were incomplete. He was very capable of that, and a lot worse. He was a wicked man, wicked from birth. He was The Devil. I wrote three papers, passed one and failed two. The two I failed were the papers no one would ever have suspected I could fail. They were my best subjects, Economics and English Literature.

My teachers launched an investigation. I don't know what they did but they concluded that something had happened to my papers. But, the damage was done. They asked me to come and repeat school. I refused. I had had enough. I went and stayed in Abakwa, where I wrote the GCE again externally and I passed. I had some of the best marks – I had an A in Literature, B in Economics, and C in History. Those were marks that the school had never had before. That year, there was no A from Nkambe in Literature. I was proud to have succeeded very well after delinking myself from the school, and from The Devil and his black magic.

It later surfaced that this man practiced his black magic or witchcraft even among his family members. We were made to understand that even the wife and the kids did not want to see him. While he was staying in Nkambe, his family avoided him like the plague by staying in the distant home village of his wife. His brother, an alcoholic, did not see eye to eye with him. They were not on talking terms when his brother died of a mysterious car accident, and The Devil did not bother to attend his funeral. He was supposedly an important notable in his home village, but his excesses of bile and bad faith meant they wanted nothing to do with him. So he was excommunicated from his village. The Devil was a very dangerous creature – a tyrant with evil powers.

Apart from the terror and tyranny of the discipline master, my high school life was good. I have some good memories from my two years in Nkambe. I remember this day when I was in lower sixth. My cousin, Ndoda, who is in Johannesburg today, was in Form Four then and staying in the dormitory. My uncle, his father, was in the shop as was his habit when not in the farm, tending cattle or attending to something else. He gave me the keys to his car – he had a bakkie –, to get his trusted driver to take Ndoda back to school. It was the end of a holiday and Ndoda was returning to the dormitory with his box of books, personal effects and food. I took the keys, I went and I didn't see the driver. Then I came back to the house and I told Ndoda, pack your things in the bakkie the driver is coming to get you. When Ndoda had packed his things, I pretended the driver was just around the corner, and asked him to enter for me to take him back to boarding school. Then I entered and started the engine.

I was very adventurous! I know I said earlier that I drove a car for the first time when I purchased my Corolla DX, but that wasn't exactly the case. That experience must have built, wittingly or otherwise, on this earlier experience when I drove Ndoda to school. The car was parked against the wall. The first thing I did was put the car in reverse. I don't know how I managed to do that. If I had got it wrong, I would have hit the wall. But I managed to put it into reverse. Then I drove up a slope and there was a main road. As I went up that slope, there came this big truck with sand. I didn't know how to stop. I swerved the car to avoid the truck. I didn't know that when you're driving, you have to hold the brakes and hold the clutch in order to stop the car. So all I did was hold the brakes, and the car stopped somewhere in the bush, narrowly avoiding a head on collision with the truck.

I reversed the car again, and frankly speaking, I drove that car to school and dropped Ndoda and came back and parked the car easily. It was quite simply magical. It was after a while that my uncle was talking with that driver, that he came to know that something had not quite happened the way he had wanted it to happen. I seemed to have caused a mechanical problem on the car. It was after some weeks that my uncle discovered while talking to the driver who was supposed to have taken Ndoda to school about an unusual noise from the car, and that the driver told him he never took George to school. My uncle came back to me. It was so embarrassing. He asked me, "I told you to tell John to take Ndoda to school, what happened? How did Ndoda go to school?" I told him I had asked a friend to take Ndoda to school when I could not find John. Immediately, I went to school to tell Ndoda what had happened, and to seek his support for my lie. My uncle still doesn't know that I drove his car that day. That was quite an incident! I used to like driving a lot. So whenever I sat in a car, I always liked to sit in front, next to the driver, so that I could watch whatever was done. And that's how I learned how to manipulate gears and things. When I bought my car, I used that knowledge I had accumulated to drive it.

Chapter 5

My Days at the University of Yaoundé

When I went to the University of Yaoundé, Cameroon still only had one university. Students still had the benefit of the scholarship or study allowance which used to be popularly known as *bourse or epsie*, even among Anglophone students. The *bourse* was paid monthly, to students who qualified to be awarded it, and qualification was usually based on how well one had performed at the GCE Advanced Level, and also on how well one continued to perform as a student at the university. Initially, my name was not on the list when I got to Yaoundé. When I was heading back for the second term, I thought my situation would remain unchanged. I prepared well, financially. I had about 50,000 francs. At the time that was big money. My father gave me 50,000 francs for my rent. I was sharing accommodation with a cousin. At the start of the second term, the second list for *bourse* awards came out and my name was there. They paid me 150,000 francs the week the list was released and the following week I was paid another 30,000 francs. This, together with the 50,000 francs that my father gave, meant that I had more than 200,000 francs in my pocket. That was the first in history, the first time ever, that I had that kind of money, and what was even more difficult to swallow was that it was all my money. That was the good thing about it. My parents never even knew that I had that money, except the 50,000 francs they had given me.

I knew fellow students, Bamileke in particular, who used the large payments of the *bourse* to start a business. Today, if you go to Ngoa-Ekelle, the neighbourhood where the university is located, there are lots of off-license bars and small shops. Some of them were started by students. Two of my classmates, they received 150,000 francs like me and they started their off-license businesses. Today they are multi-millionaires. They opened these drinking places where they hired girls to sell food and drinks, and before they knew it, their money had multiplied, and hasn't stopped multiplying since then.

As for me, I didn't do much with my own pay-out. I had this clique, a group of friends, with whom I used to drink. We had a favourite drinking place where we could go and drink even when we did not have the money to pay immediately. There was a big ledger in which the owner would write our names and what we owed him. We were a group of five. We were so familiar with this bar that everyone serving there knew our choices. We ordered our beer in crates. I used to drink, indiscriminately. I mixed everything. I would start with Mutziig, then move to Satzenbrau and 33 Export, to end up with Guinness. I would enter the bar, order drinks, empty bottle after bottle as I stood, and only on the fifth bottle would I look for a seat. That's how bad it was. With my mates, there were instances when we would have five crates in front of us. It was our understanding that the slowest or the last person to finish drinking was the one to settle the bill. We drank as if we were cursed.

So when I had my pay-out of *bourse*, my mates were there for us to carry drinking to another level. When we had drank at our regular bar, and there was still that much money to spend I decided to take on another challenge for the weekend. My uncle in Douala was getting married. That was a perfect excuse for me to seek a change in drinking venue. Once in Douala, I identified a bar in a New Layout quarter in the Bassa area, where a couple of my relatives lived, along with many others from Pinyin. Here we continued drinking. All we ate was meat.

We drank so much alcohol that on Sunday, the day of the wedding, I was unable to attend. I had to sleep. You can't cheat nature. On Monday, I went to the market and bought myself a leather jacket and nice shoes, and I went back to Yaoundé. I practiced some very bad habits in Yaoundé. It was Friday, so I took a bus to Douala. I had all of the money in my pocket. In Douala, we continued drinking, all weekend. I finished that money like that. I finished it. It was finished; I could not even buy text books or the polycopies that professors used to compile for sale. That's where my money went. I poured it all into drink. I still regret it today.

The government was good at the time, giving out such bursaries. But some of us were reckless as well. I think it was because of that money that I became a drunkard. I used to drink a lot. At that time it was normal because every other person was drinking. Everywhere was one big sea of alcohol, parcelled out in bars and off-licenses, peopled with thirsting consumers who desired nothing short of their staple – the standard and popular beers of Cameroon. Sometimes, as a spendthrift myself, I seriously doubted the extent to which Cameroonians were able to save any of the money they made, when alcohol had such a lure and charm on us.

When, eventually, I stopped drinking and stopped smoking – because it finally dawned on me that I used to spend a lot on these two things – I was suddenly able to save, and did so significantly. Drinking and smoking have a way with our money that is almost unnoticeable until it is too late.

As someone who lives outside of Cameroon and only visits occasionally these days, I am struck by how much people cry and complain of poverty. But if you check how much alcohol the very same people consume on a daily basis, if you check how much money they waste on things that are not important, you'll see that people are not poor in Cameroon, they're not poor at all. It is this culture of wasteful expenditure that cripples the country and its people. I don't know when this will stop. Personally, I stopped it and was able to make something out of my life. But collectively, we have much unfinished business with drinking and our culture of waste. It really bothers me; when you go to Cameroon and see people drink, they smoke and they beg, people are so dishonest with money. We are made to feel guilty if we don't harken to the cry of desperate relatives and friends back home. But what happens to the money when you do? What do they do with the money? They just drink. Elsewhere we hear of miracles transforming water into wine, but in Cameroon you don't need a miracle to transform money into urine.

This culture of drinking in Cameroon has actually gone overboard, but I don't know how we can stop it. When you talk to people, they retort what do you expect them to do in their circumstances? It seems like drinking has been enshrined as a solution that does not really resolve any of the myriad problems Cameroonians face as individuals and as a society. Beer has become a placebo cure to Biya. Yet, personally, I wonder how true that excuse is. I think people just want to drink. My life in the university was like that, just drinking, and I could resort to any reason to justify my drinking. I drank a lot. I drank to cool down, drank to warm up, drank to keep busy, drank to stay still, drank to keep boredom at bay, drank to welcome friends, drank to send friends off, drank because I craved the thrills of being tipsy or drunk, and drank to de-drunk myself. There was always a reason and an excuse to drink. I don't know what changed me. When I didn't drink, I was just a guy, in fact I was a gentleman. But in university, I started drinking publicly because I had the money. You know at one stage in your life you have to venture. But I had bad friends as well.

One thing that stands out with my university education is that, even though I was drinking, I never failed any examination. I had three June successes. I never repeated a class or subject. I just used to pass. When I went out drinking, I would return home and go straight to study and do my assignments while my drinking partners would go and sleep. I used to be that kind of person who didn't need to read a lot to do my best. I didn't read a lot but I used to pass. So I did my three years and I had my first degree. I qualified to do the *maîtrise* – Honours –, but I never wanted to do it.

Bula was one of my drinking partners, a home boy, friend and class mate from High School, who did more post-drinking reading than me. He became doctor of law. But he is of late now. He was quite intelligent, but he had to read and read before he could pass his exams. He must read. But I was not like that. He used to drink just like me. The one thing that I remember is that every single day, after we had been drinking and had gotten back, Bula never sat on the bed, he sat on the chair and read. He read till dawn, then took a bath and went to school. After my hour or so of reading, I would go to sleep, and he would have to wake me to go to class with him, as we were in the same class and stayed together. I only stayed awake when the exams timetable was up. Together with Bula, we would burn the midnight oil. The only thing permitted to interrupt our reading then was eating.

I remember Bula as a very straight forward person who did not mince his words. Even though we had the *bourse*, our reckless drinking meant that sometimes we found ourselves without food, especially after paying our rents, for the cost of accommodation was very high. One day we were particularly hungry when Bula asked me in these words that have stayed with me forever, "You say Zunka is your cousin. How come we are suffering here – we don't have anything to eat – and he's got so much; he's driving a nice car, staying in a nice house and you don't go to ask him to give us some money?" My answer to him was simple: "I don't beg. That's not my nature."

Still he insisted we go to his office the following day. So we did. We went to my cousin's office. We went in. Bula led the way. We went in, sat. I couldn't talk. I couldn't ask him anything. Bula took the initiative. He explained to him: "Sir. You know it is difficult. We don't have food at home. We don't have food to eat. This is exam time. We have nothing. So please give us some money." That was the way he talked. Straight! "Give us some money, we need some money." My cousin gave us some money indeed! He gave us 2000 francs!!!! Even in those days 2000 francs had little value. When we came out of the office, I lambasted Bula for pushing me to riddle myself. Bula apologized to me. He was truly discouraged. He agreed with me that it is better to turn to a friend than to go to someone that mean in the name of family. When I was going to university, my father gave me only 50,000 francs, reminding me that I had a brother in Yaoundé who was a big man in government, and who had lots of money. He instructed me to go to meet him whenever I needed financial assistance. I knew my cousin better to bother. Without Bula and his insistence, I would have left Yaoundé without ever having to pass by my elite cousin. Another cousin of mine also at the university who insisted in taking these relationships at face value, would visit this distinguished elitist big man cousin of ours repeatedly only to complain after every visit that he was seldom given food to eat, paid attention by the big man or asked if he had money for taxi or the bus. Why on earth he kept going, I never fathomed.

My ex-wife was with me at university. She was a positive influence in my life in so many ways. If I studied hard and thought about my future it was because of her. It came to a point that, after the birth of Taanji, our first child, she always told me that I had brought an innocent soul into the world and that, even if we were not going to get married, we owe him the responsibility to be decent in whatever we could be, including in our thoughts about the future. I still remember she used to tell me things like that to motivate me. It could be that without the influence of this girl I would have just gone deeper and deeper into drinking and bad friends and total failure. But because of her, I had this sense of responsibility. She always made me understand that we needed to proceed with care and foresight.

I think that's the positive thing that she brought to my life. Even though most of these things that I used to do, I used to hide from her. Our relationship was not smooth. When she became pregnant, it was really tough, it was difficult. The family never really wanted me. She grew up with an auntie who was very strict. The auntie never wanted to see a man come to the house or see her niece associating with a man. We hid the relationship for some time. But when she became pregnant and a child was involved, we couldn't hide it anymore. Her family didn't know I was the father of the baby until the baby was actually born. They knew me as a friend, as a school mate, but not as a boyfriend to their daughter. Babies are from God. When she had the baby, I was in second year and she was in her first year at university. We were both in the first year when she got pregnant towards the end of the first year, and because of that she didn't get promoted to second year. She went to Abakwa to have the baby. When the baby was a few months old, she left him in Abakwa with Anna, her cousin, and came back to Yaoundé to continue with her studies. No one knew that I was the father of the baby, not even Anna, who only knew me as a friend. Anna had been very supportive towards Taanji's mother even in Yaoundé where she just completed her studies. She actually became Taanji's mother in every sense of the word until he moved to South Africa. Anna is a very loving and a lovable person and remains a true friend till date. When I visited them in Abakwa, Anna was holding Taanji in her arms when I came into the house. The baby was just a few months old. Something happened. This baby started pinching her, like it was wanting to go down. The baby could not crawl. But when Anna placed the baby down, the baby mumbled "papa", "papa", and started crawling to me. That was the first word that Taanji uttered, and that is when everyone knew I was the father. It's the baby who revealed me to everyone. I picked Taanji up and felt the warmth of being close to my flesh and blood, my son. I had this feeling that I have never felt again since that day. I don't know how to describe the feeling, but it felt so good, so right.

Anna is hard working. She used to be very hard working. Even when she was pregnant, her work did not suffer. And she never deterred from seeking to put me on the right path, especially with my heavy drinking. I hate to think, with the benefit of hindsight, that I did not prioritise the essential things of life when I got my lump sum *bourse*. She would not have had to fend for herself during holidays to take care of the pregnancy and the baby, eventually. Her family and friends never wanted to hear anything about the baby, and several of them tried to persuade her to have an abortion. But she refused. She never wanted to listen to the parents about the baby. She was a tenacious woman. When I graduated from the university and left Yaoundé to practice law in Abakwa, she was still to start her third year, having delayed her studies by a year to have the baby.

When I finally became known as the father of her son, it was the turn of my parents to develop cold feet. She comes from a faraway village known as Mbesa. I come from Pinyin; and the Pinyin people by nature are very tribalistic. It became so difficult for my parents to acknowledge or accept her into the family. It was tough. Even when we finally got married, I did it on my own. My parents only started accepting her after we got together. But again, sometimes parents might be right. Parents might be right because at the end of the day, what they used to tell me came to pass. But that's another story.

Chapter 6

Saudi Arabia Beckons

I had a friend who was a Muslim in Old Town, Abakwa. He used to tell me how good it was in Saudi Arabia. I knew little about that country, and things were not as easy to find out in those days as they are today with the Internet and with Google. But this friend told me how Saudi Arabia is one of the gulf countries; how it's got a lot of oil and they've got a lot of minerals, and that there are so many jobs there. It just occurred to me that it was better to leave Cameroon and settle somewhere else. I decided to leave for Saudi Arabia. But then, the problem was, how was I to get there?

The same friend told me that it was better for me to become a Muslim and then to join the Hajj group for a pilgrimage to Mecca. The intention was for me to stay there after. So that's what I did. I converted to Islam. Then I joined one of the groups. I made a passport and gave it to the leader of the group who got me a visa to go for the Hajj. That was actually my first trip out of Cameroon. I was travelling to an Islamic country. I was supposed to be a Muslim, but my being Muslim was only in principle. I did not even know how to pray as a Muslim, yet I was travelling to Mecca to participate in the Hajj as a devout Muslim. I used to be called James. In preparation for Mecca, I took on the name Jibraeel, giving up my English name of James, a name I had taken on when I was baptized and confirmed as a Christian. It was only much later when I started to familiarize myself with the Koran that I became aware that James actually translates into Jibraeel. Otherwise, I was not a practicing Muslim, and didn't know how to pray when we boarded the Cameroonian Airline flight in Douala and took off for Saudi Arabia. I hadn't the foggiest idea of what to expect, since I had never ventured outside of Cameroon before.

I did have the feeling though, of moving from one small place to a bigger one. At the airport in Douala, I suddenly felt the magnitude of what I was taking on. This was actually something big. I was at the airport, and I was travelling out of the country. It was a real sense of achievement, when we finally arrived at the Hajj Terminal of Jeddah King Abdulaziz International Airport in Saudi Arabia. Compared to Saudi Arabia, Cameroon was like a village. The airport was beyond description. It was big. It was like a different world. Wow!!! That's the feeling I had. I thought I was in a different world. I thought it was unlike where I came from, and unlike Douala airport. This was simply a wonder beyond words. If you compared the airport in Jeddah with the International Airport in Douala, the airport in Douala could pass for an airstrip in the backyard of someone's house in Saudi Arabia. That's what I thought in my mind.

From Jeddah we went the road of pilgrims. The only thing I remembered when I left Cameroon was that I was told in Saudi Arabia there's no alcohol, they don't smoke cigarettes and they don't do drugs. So I expected to get to Saudi Arabia and live this life of chastity and purity, especially given the fact that I had matured into a giant of a smoker – a moving chimney of sorts. At the airport in Douala, I smoked what I thought was my last cigarette. But I was so surprised when I was coming down from the plane at the Jeddah airport that the first person who came to welcome us was smoking. I exclaimed my relief in silence. I tried to imagine how on earth I was going to quit smoking just like that, because, as I had been made to understand, there were no cigarettes in Saudi Arabia, and smoking was severely disallowed.

Upon seeing him smoking, I felt the urge to smoke. I couldn't speak Arabic, and he didn't understand English when I asked him for a cigarette. So we used sign language. I made the sign of a cigarette and smoking and he gave me one, which I smoked. I said "wow!" It wasn't as bad as I thought. Feeling wholesome again, I went with the others for the Hajj. We did all the pilgrimage rites. We went to Muzdalifah, Mina, Arafat, Migat Territory, where pilgrims cleanse themselves before entering Makkah. We lodged in Makkah for some time and from there we visited the Great Mosque, Sa'i Area, Tawaf Area, Jamarat Area etc. We went to all those places and performed all hajj rites. Gradually I was being converted to Islam. I started enjoying the life and I started making an effort to learn how to pray and gradually it had an effect on me. I must say that I really enjoyed Islam while I was in Saudi Arabia and I actually became a practicing Muslim during my stay.

While I discovered many myths about Saudi Arabia, I also discovered some truths about it. The one truth I realized about Saudi Arabia was that men and women don't mix. The men stay apart from the women in everything that is done. In the hotels, on the buses, in taxis: women and men must be apart. The buses in Saudi Arabia are double-deckers, with an entrance for men and another for women. From what I saw, the men would go upstairs and the ladies would stay down stairs. Even when a man comes face to face with a woman, the woman is completely veiled – she does not show flesh; women put on gloves, they put on socks, and the woman's face cannot be seen.

I had this experience when I visited the home of a Saudi. He was the owner of the company that I eventually worked for. When we arrived at his house, I realized that there was a dining section that was hidden from view. When you walked into the lounge, there were thick curtains that separated the dining section that was kept from the public view. That was done to keep women from the eye of the public, because they didn't want women to serve food from the same table as the men and especially visitors. Women could serve food for the men to eat, without being noticed, and ring a bell to indicate that food was ready, without being visible. There was no communication. When my host heard the bell, he knew food was ready and would then invite us to go and eat.

My host was married with daughters, but you didn't see them. Even on TV, when I put on the TV, it was rare that one saw women. Only once in a while did you see a woman on TV, as a presenter or doing an interview, but they were always veiled. The rarity of women's faces was so acute that even if you are looking to be married in Saudi Arabia - a man seeking a woman - the woman is never met face to face. You advertise in a newspaper, on the radio or television, you leave your phone number and your photo. Today, with the advent of the cell phone and social media like Facebook, I can imagine the increased availability of avenues for men and women to discover one another outside the façade of what one can or cannot display or perform in public as a woman and between men and women. That is of course in the absence of censorship on social media in that country.

In those days, without these technologies of instant availability and reachability, the women interested in getting married or just in a relationship would contact you. Then, it is only after a long time of communicating with the family and with the woman, and only when all agree on the relationship, that the day comes when a meeting between the two is set up. . You go to the woman's house and they will unveil the woman for you to see her face. That was something that was a bit strange to me, coming from Cameroon where things are done differently. But now that I am familiar with Islam, I know that in Islam we believe that men must be disciplined. Sex crimes are encouraged due to the fact that women expose themselves, because a man naturally responds to sight and touch. So they want to keep sex crimes at bay. I think that's one of the reasons, and the other reason is in the Koran itself. It was a practice of Mohamed's teachings that women should not be exposed. That's the life practicing Muslims live, even here in Cape Town. Look at practicing Muslims everywhere. The women are always veiled.

After the pilgrimage, I officially added another name to my name repertoire; Alhaji: James Jibraeel Alhaji. Today different people call me different names; James, Jibraeel, Alhaji, Jib, Jimmy, Pa Penn, etc. I have come in contact with so many people in my journey through life, so much so that it becomes difficult to recognize most of them when we meet again. So the name they call me by makes it easier to locate more or less where and when we knew each other and thereby helps me to recognize them and relate with them easily.

After the Hajj to Makkah, I decided to stay on in Saudi Arabia when the pilgrims from Cameroon were coming back. That was the reason I went to Saudi Arabia in the first place. It was difficult for me. How do I stay illegally? I had to abandon my group, leave the airport and go into town. We were back in Jeddah, at the Hajj Terminal of the airport. It was the first time I ventured into breaking the law. I didn't have the right visa to stay in Saudi Arabia after the pilgrimage, so I had to find my way out of the airport and into the city illegally. It was a scary thing to do. The authorities couldn't let me go into town without a visa. So I contacted a guy, a black guy, whom I met there. You always find people like that when the chips are down. I've forgotten whether this guy was a Nigerian or Ghanaian, but he was a guy who had been in Saudi Arabia for quite a while. He was a Muslim. So I met this guy and I told him my intentions. He could barely understand English but at least he understood me. He said he was going to help me. Although I had the lingering feeling that we didn't understand each other properly, I knew, somehow, that he was going to help me out of the airport. Where I would go from there, I didn't know.

He was going ahead, I followed him. He took my bag. I had a small bag with a few clothes inside. Then there were four barb wired, iron fences. To get to the road at a distance where I could see cars passing, I had to jump over those four barb wired and iron fences combined.

It was tough. The guy just insisted I follow him. So I followed him. He threw my bag over the fence, and we climbed up and over. His eyes were sharp and everywhere. It was important to check first, then make a move, which he did like someone who used to do just that for a living. There were policemen who were patrolling the parameters, but we were helped by the fact that it was night. The police always checked this area. We finally succeeded in jumping over all four fences, got to the main road, and then walked a distance to where we got a taxi. The taxi we stopped was a meter taxi. I didn't understand Arabic, and depended fully on the guy with me .

He took me somewhere. It was a house where there were black people. It was like a hostel and there were Ghanaians and Nigerians there. There were no Cameroonians. There were only Ghanaians and Nigerians staying in that place and one of them could speak good English, so we started communicating and I discovered to my greatest dismay that those guys, all those black guys staying there, were illegal immigrants and some of them had been staying there for five or ten years, and they never had legal papers. That is when I started being discouraged. I started asking myself if that was the right move, if I did the right thing coming to Saudi Arabia.

It was so dangerous going round town. They knew the times that they could move, and so I let them guide me around. I had some money, in dollars, which I changed into Riyal, the local currency. With that I was able to subsist and to hire a taxi when we went out. I was desperate to connect with a Cameroonian in order to have a sense what Saudi Arabia was from the experience of someone whose background or origins were close to mine. So the guy who had helped me out of the airport again took me there, where I met the representative of Cameroon Airlines. The latter was so nice to us. I spoke to him nicely and he was very friendly. He was Cameroonian from the North Province, as the current North Region was known then. I told him I did law at university, and we actually communicated. I asked him about the possibilities of getting a job in Saudi Arabia, of settling there, and he gave me tips, although I did not tell him that it was my intention at the time to stay in the country. I asked him to take me to the Cameroon Airlines office at the airport. He took me there, I met the person in charge, and I told him the truth. He was very sympathetic with me and my situation. The Representative of Camair later on took me to his house, and that's where I stayed for the six months that I was in Saudi Arabia. He remains one of those good Samaritans I would most love to reconnect with, but unfortunately, I have searched for him everywhere, googled and visited websites without relent, but with no luck. That was when Cameroon Airlines was still functioning. It just so happens that some people who help you, you never find them again. But I haven't given up trying, especially as my sophistication in combing the internet is growing by the day. If he is there somewhere, a search engine or another will unearth him one day.

He was such a nice guy. He gave me a job. The founder of the company that I worked for was his personal friend. I never had papers but he got me a job. I was a translator for the company, which was an import and export company. They were importing fruits and cash crops from Africa into Saudi Arabia and they were dealing with African countries but they didn't have links with Cameroon. So they wanted someone who could at least translate for them, when they received communications from French speaking countries. A few of them in the company had studied in the US, so English was the only international language they knew outside of Arabic. No one in the company spoke a word of French. So I became the official translator of the company, French – English, English – French. If they needed to draft letters, I did it for them, they provided me with documents. My French was not good but I had to do it. I was the translator. As the saying goes, in the kingdom of the blind, the one-eyed is king. For six months and without papers, I worked there. The Cameroonian I was staying with had to take me in his car when he was going to work, and would drop me off at work at the company, and then continue to work. Then the founder of the company would drop me off at home after work. If he was not going to work, if he was out of town, the founder of the company would send a car to come and take me because I could not go on my own transport, for fear of being intercepted by the immigration police. I survived for six months, but it was so difficult not having papers.

I was saving most of my salary. I earned much better than I would have done in Cameroon, but I couldn't stay any longer. I couldn't stay after those six months, the life was intolerable. Imagine someone who came from a Christian background. I was a party animal. I used to go to pubs, go to parties and I used to socialize with women. In Saudi Arabia, I could not even see a woman, I could not drink beer, I could not go to places, and I was missing my family back home. The worse one was that I was not free to move around. I was like a prisoner. I felt under arrest. I could not do what I wanted, even though I had everything – I was living in a nice house. I was made to understand that things are a little different in Riyadh, at least for Americans. Apparently, in Riyadh there is an American village. Americans are predominantly Christians and they have got a lot of interest in Saudi Arabia. Because the life that they live in Saudi Arabia is not the life that Americans live, they have created an American village to enable Americans to do their things away from the watchful or envious eye of the Saudis. Americans like to drink. They like to go after women. They like partying. But that's not the way of life in Saudi Arabia. Hence the special authorization of the government to create what they call an American village in Riyadh. In this village you could drink alcohol, and go free, there you could visit prostitutes, and so on. It is like life in America but only within that small area. Despite this leeway, anyone who commits a crime outside of this confinement and is caught is punished just like any other criminal. If they catch you committing fornication or adultery, they either kill you or they stone you to death. If they catch you with drugs, they cut off your finger or your hand. Those were the laws in Saudi Arabia

The wife of my host was back in Cameroon, and we had a big house all to ourselves. We had such a big house, such a big swimming pool. There was a cook, and there was a cleaner. In those days, Cameroon used to lavish money on its workers, especially those recruited and posted abroad, like my friend of Cameroon Airlines. I remember one day I was in that big house all by myself. My friend had gone out, and so had the cook. There was no one else in the compound but me. It was really hot, almost 40 degrees. I went to the pool to freshen up. I didn't know it was that deep! I thought to myself, a pool inside a house, how could I drown inside a house? The deepness took me by surprise. I almost drowned. I was under the water. I didn't know how to move. Water was forcing itself down my throat through my mouth and nostrils. I could have been under water for many minutes. But God was good. My kicks of desperation managed to get me somewhere and I discovered I could stand on my feet above the water. I came out of the pool and I lay on the ground panting. It was such a bad experience. I swore to never do that again. I don't know how long I was lying in that place trying to squeeze the water out of me before the cleaner came. I was very weak. I could have died. When the cleaner arrived, he helped me take out the water and gave me some medication. I couldn't even go to the hospital. I was an illegal immigrant: hospitals are not the place for such people. Blacks are rare and easily spotted in Saudi Arabia. They can spot a black man from one kilometre away. That's how bad it was being black and an illegal immigrant in that country. Going out into town was very dangerous and when they caught you, they took you in. Your sentence was deportation, and if you were lucky you were put in jail. It was dangerous. Hardly my idea of freedom!

That's the reason that I decided I better go back to Cameroon. I decided to go back to meet my family in Cameroon, and maybe continue with my Nigerian business. To facilitate my exit from the country, the Cameroon Airlines manager did certain documents, and he actually accompanied me to the flight. I didn't understand Arabic, so I don't know what he told the authorities. He's the one who made things easier for me.

Wonders shall never end. I gave the car I bought before leaving for Saudi Arabia to one of my cousins who was a driver, and we agreed he was going to drive it as a taxi and give money to my then fiancée, Taanji's mother. On the evening of my departure this cousin had a ghastly accident at Finance

Junction Nkwen with that car. The damage was a lot and the guy was badly injured. I was to leave Abakwa the following day at about 7 o'clock, so all I could do was tow the car to a garage where I left it. While I was away, I managed to have the car fixed. That's another story. When I decided to come back to Cameroon and establish myself as a businessman again, thinking like a businessman would, I knew it would be silly of me to carry money on me back to Cameroon. I remembered that during the Hajj I had seen people buying lots of jewellery and clothing. So I decided to buy some jewellery, clothing and other items I believed I could sell in Cameroon, with the money that I had saved and took off to Cameroon.

On the plane on my way back, I met this guy who had lived and worked in Riyadh for several years. I guess he was working at the Cameroon consulate in Riyadh. During the time that he was in Saudi Arabia, he never tasted alcohol but he was a Christian. There was free alcohol in the plane, beer, wine and spirits. Having stayed in Saudi Arabia for such a long time, and not drinking alcohol, this guy decided to go on a drinking spree in the plane. I can still see him drinking. He didn't even eat. All he did was drink. He drank and drank, and when the alcohol was not forthcoming, he would go and abuse the hostesses and take alcohol from the kitchenette. By the time he got to Douala, he could not recognize anyone anymore. The police took him and kept him somewhere until he came to. That is what life in Saudi Arabia can do to someone.

I got back to Cameroon. My troubles started again. The merchandise I bought I had bought without thinking about how I was going to sell it all. So, I gave them out to people who promised to pay in instalments. But as is often the case with such a way of business, I lost almost all of the money that I had earned in Saudi Arabia under the most difficult conditions for six months. I gave out jewellery, dresses, and clothing, for people who said they were going to sell and pay me. It was a lot of money. I have forgotten just how much. I didn't even recover ¼ of the money. The car I had left in Cameroon for business, the one I had toiled and sent money back to be repaired, was another headache. It continued to deliver more headaches than profit, as drivers engineered ever more fabulous accounts instead of bringing home the money that the car was meant to generate. Even when drivers managed and brought a little money, my brother would take the money and do his own things with it. Not even a dime was saved for me, the owner of the damn car! I concluded that it is good for one to do one's business by oneself.

I came back. I did not tell them that I was coming back. I came back to meet that car suspended, driven with reckless abandon and without any attention to the need to maintain it. They were not servicing the car so it was in bad shape. I tried to resurrect the car. It worked. So I started driving it again as a taxi. I became a taxi driver in Abakwa. All the money that I brought from Saudi Arabia was gone. I started driving, and decided to take that car to the South West because that's where I was based before I left. I knew that area better than Abakwa, businesswise.

In the South West I started doing what we called *"fungeh"* at the time. This was the name given to illegally imported or smuggled petrol from Nigeria. I started trading in *Fungeh*, using the car to transport it from places like Edenau to Victoria and beyond. It was a lucrative business, but it was also a business where one had lots of tussles with the police and other forces of law and order, during which you could lose a lot of money. Sometimes you can even make 100,000 francs on it. But that was when I had the second car. I had a bakkie. There's an uncle of mine, my mother's junior brother, he had a Toyota Hilux that was damaged. It wasn't running when he retired from the army so he tried to fix the bakkie. At the time I was doing *fungeh* in the South West, so I told him it would be good to bring the car to the South West so that I could transport *fungeh* and the car could pay the debts it owed. I took it down to the South West and added it to my Corolla. From then, I had 2 vehicles to do business with.

The worst thing about *fungeh* was that you could make 100,000 francs today and tomorrow you spend 150,000 francs, because it was an illegal business. The gendarmes would take your car, the police would take your car and the customs would take your car. That's how it is in Cameroon – so many people doing the same thing. Whether it was the army, the customs, the police or gendarmes that took your car, each of them had a fixed amount of money that they expected you to pay them to set you and your car free. For the customs, it was 200,000 francs, for the gendarmes it was 150,000 francs or so, and 100,000 francs for the police. Often, they went after your cars because they wanted that money.

If you didn't want to go and pay those standard charges because they are exorbitant, you could bribe them with much less. At the customs I had my classmate, Acha. He was my godfather . Whenever the customs took my car, I would call him even at midnight, and go to his house. He would go and take the car out and give it back to me. So with the customs I had no problem. Then I also had someone at the gendarmerie. I made those relationships as time went on. I discovered the commandant of the gendarmerie in Victoria afterwards. He was someone I knew when I was at high school in Nkambe. He was the commandant of the Brigade there. He was of Douala origin. He used to love women so much and we used to meet in the nightclub. I used to be his agent, someone he would commission or ask to bring his girlfriends from high school for him. When I discovered that he was the one in charge of the gendarmerie in Victoria, I knew that no one could touch me. As for the police on the other hand, the commissioner of police, Mr Ngem, fell in love with me. He had attended the University of Yaoundé, just like me, graduating two years before I did. He understood the plight of those of us who came after them. There were no jobs. When I was still at the law chambers struggling to join the bar association, he was friends with my boss. So he knew me from there as well. With those connections, at least I was secured in Victoria. Then if I moved out of Victoria I had my godfather in the magistrate in Tiko, Mr. Nkeng, a tribesman from Ngali. Today he is the president of the Appeal Court in Abakwa. I was well protected. That's why I wanted to be in Victoria. I knew people there. In order for you to do things in Cameroon you must know people. I became quite connected, and made a lot of money.

This was a business that had sustained many jobless degree holders. One of my closest friends here in Cape Town, Anyu, we came here together, and were together in the *Fungeh* business in Victoria prior to our departure for South Africa.

At one time there was an anti-gang squad that came from Yaoundé to put an end to the trade in *fungeh*. They didn't know anyone. They surprised the police, the gendarmes, and the customs. They were taking orders from Yaoundé. There was no way that dealers in *Fungeh* like myself could get the protection they were used to getting, using the networks and contacts we had forged with the various forces of law and order. So the anti-gang from Yaoundé killed that business. They actually put an end to that business. That is what forced me to start going to Nigeria again. They took my car. They were stationed in Man O War Bay, not far from Victoria, along the sea. The roads leading there are so bad. They took both my cars to Man O War Bay. All the money I had saved up, I had to spend in taking the cars out of their possession. I can't remember how much money I spent to take care of those cars, but it was a very big amount. To corrupt the anti-gang squad was not easy. They were francophones from Yaoundé, and they had expressed orders and they were soldiers with a mission. However, I found a way to take one of the cars. The situation of the other car was more complicated, as I found out. It seemed that car had been taken to the gendarmerie instead. At the time my friend the commandant was not in town, and the guys who were charged with custody of the car were ready to strip me of all the protection I was used to having. I had to pay quite some money to reclaim it. I spent all the money I had saved up, and there was no more *Fungeh* for me to make the money back. My days of lucrative business were gone, and with it the money that I had made.

It was while doing the *Fungeh* business that I was detained in a police cell for the first time in my life. The conditions in the cell were deplorable. It was a small room of 2m by 2m, and it was so packed full of people that there was hardly room for anyone to sit. We only had space to stand. To make matters worse, it was the dry season, and the heat and humidity in Victoria at that time of the year is beyond imagination. There was no window. I stood throughout the night, unable to even lean against the wall. It was a very bad experience. The following day the commissioner came and took me out, but the damage had been done. That day taught me that you must be afraid of the cell in Cameroon. It is bad, really bad.

The second time I was detained, it was in the gendarmerie – that was better. When the trade in *Fungeh* was banned, I decided to start trading with Nigeria again. I decided now to sell my Corolla DX. One of the big guns in the *Fungeh* trade bought the car. The car was still under gendarmerie custody when he bought it. The idea was for him to pay me so I could go and pay the gendarmerie to release the car. The only balance

I was left with from selling the car and settling the gendarmerie was about 200,000 francs. The car was worth 1,500,000 francs at the time, but I was forced to sell it for much cheaper because of the difficulty I found myself in. I think I sold it for about 600,000 francs, if I am not mistaken. The complication came in the fact that the money the buyer paid me for the car included counterfeit 10,000 francs banknotes. Without knowing at the time, I took the money, went to the gendarmerie to give them the huge bribe that they insisted I owed them, so I could collect my car and hand over to the person who had bought it. When the gendarmes counted the money, they discovered the counterfeit notes, and took me in. I had to tell them from whom I got the money, so they took the name, went and picked him up as well. Both of us were locked up. The following day I got out of there, and I decided to go back to Nigeria to start trading the way I had before. I decided to venture out of Cameroon to Saudi Arabia.

The reason for selling the car was to raise money so as to go to Nigeria. The money that I got was not enough, so I had to borrow more. At that time I had a contract with one new private hospital in Yaoundé, where I was supposed to supply hospital equipment, including surgery beds, laboratory equipment like microscopes and other accessories. It was a contract worth a lot of money – 25 million francs to be exact. I was supposed to supply the equipment in two instalments. My idea was to go for the first consignment, supply them and then collect the money to go for the final consignment. To start, I had to raise something like seven million francs, which was quite difficult to get at the time. I didn't succeed in raising the full amount, but with the little money that I got, I went. I can't remember how much it was – from the sale of the car, some savings and borrowing from friends as well. I went to Nigeria. Normally I used to go to Nigeria by boat, from Ngeme beach, and it normally used to pass through the Bakassi area.

It was not my first trip to Nigeria by sea. I knew it was going to take five hours to get there and five hours to come back. Five hours to the first town in Nigeria, then I had to take transport to Onitsha where I would do my buying. I went, bought everything, came back to the border town, and loaded everything on to the boat. It was a big boat. All of those things amounted to my life savings, amounted to everything I had. That was everything I had and more, because I had to indebt myself to buy those things. What I was thinking about was the 25 million that I was going to make. I calculated that for me to make 25 million I didn't need to spend more than 12 million. It was quite a good business. So it was a trip that I was very anxious about doing.

As I have said, it normally takes five hours on the boat between Victoria and the Nigerian border town where we alight, but the boat on this particular trip back was not in a hurry to reach Victoria. It were three days at sea. It was very rough in the sea, and because the sea was rough, the engine of the boat was running all the time. We could not progress to Cameroon. When the sea is rough it is the waves that direct the boat, you don't go in the direction you intended. The boat went up to a point where the petrol ran out in the high seas. We didn't know where we were. We sat in the boat and watched the waves go higher and higher, higher than a house, coming towards us. That's how dangerous it was. We had to use buckets to carry water that came into the boat and throw it back out into the seas, to avoid the boat from sinking. But that only lasted for a while. There was this wave that came and, I don't know whether there was a hole somewhere in the boat or what. Water just kept on coming into the boat and it started sinking. The pilot, or the driver of the boat or whatever we used to call them, told us the only way to save our lives was to take everything on board and throw it overboard, to stop the boat from sinking.

I took microscopes and surgery beds and other equipment with my own hands and threw them into the sea, never to see them again, everything! Everything! I mean everything! But thank God we were safe. I think it was the third day in the sea, we found ourselves close to Equatorial Guinea, to Malabo. Because there was no petrol, the boat was just floating, drifting, and it was a fisher man from Equatorial Guinea who came to our aid. He discovered us in the sea, inquired what our problem was, and went and brought petrol to us. It was then that we finally arrived back in Victoria.

Photos

James Jibraeel Alhaji, Family and Friends

J.J. Alhaji and his three sons above
&
with his South African wife below

With Friends

with wife above & colleague below

Early Days in South Africa

In traditional Cameroonian outfit

Father and members of family in Cameroon

Mother's Burial in Alhaji's absence above

With Mother and siblings below

At a Cameroonian party in Cape Town

Relaxing in Cape Town

Keeping Business Records

At a Training Session above & below in Muslim outfit

Out and about in winter in Cape Town

Earlier High School & University Days in Cameroon in below

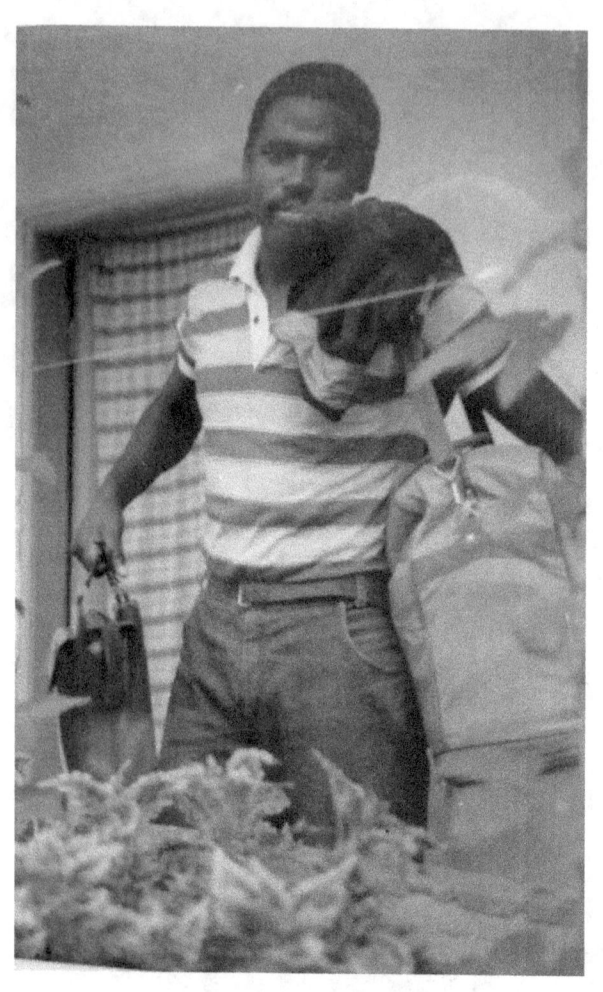

Chapter 7

South Africa Imagined and Pursued

When I landed in Victoria it was like my world had just ended in Cameroon. My life just ended because there was nothing I could call my own. I didn't even have enough money to eat. I didn't even have money to pay my rents. That's how bad it was. The worse thing was that I owed people. I had debts. It was at that juncture that I discovered that there's nothing more to do in Cameroon. If I insisted that Cameroon was still the place to be, where was I to start putting things together all over again? How would I go about paying my debts? Where would I get the money to start any business again? These were questions I couldn't answer. I was sick and tired of being too trusting to Cameroon, a country that was reluctant to open doors for me. I still had with me the old Toyota Hilux. I decided to sell it and leave Cameroon.

The idea of South Africa had always been on my mind since my return from Saudi Arabia. I would go down and take the atlas and draw my itinerary on how I would go to South Africa. I used to do that with my friend Anyu, who is here in Cape Town as well. We travelled together. I had completed the journey from Cameroon to South Africa over a thousand times in my imagination. I used to sit and draw myself leaving Cameroon, going through Congo Brazzaville, Zaire or Congo Kinshasa (today's Democratic Republic of Congo (DRC), Zambia, Zimbabwe and South Africa. Later on, this dream paper itinerary was to change. So the idea was to sell my old Toyota Hilux and make this imagination come true. I found someone who was interested in my car, and agreed with him to pay me 700,000 francs. He gave me an advanced payment of

200,000 francs, and said he didn't really have any more money. So I arranged for him to pay that money to my friend Chuh. The idea was that Chuh would use the money to pay some of my debts. Till today, nearly twenty years later, the man is yet to pay a cent of the 500,000 francs that he owes me.

I struggled and got an additional 100,000 francs from Lafah, a childhood friend who was like a brother, and who has always been there for me. That made a total of 300,000 francs for my adventure to South Africa. When I started trading in reagents the very first time I went to Nigeria Lafah also contributed part of the money towards the capital that I needed at the time. He worked with an insurance company and was used to helping me when I was down. He was like that. He was a true friend, a brother. We went through good and bad times together. We always had each other's back. I could write a book on our life memories. Today he's in the US. We kept the friendship alive via the phone and social media for a long while. But sometimes out of sight is out of mind. He has been in the US for so many years. I left him in Cameroon then for my South Africa adventure. The only time I saw him again was when I went back to Cameroon in January 2012. He lost his father and came for the funeral celebrations and I also came for my father's memorial. It was quite a moving meeting, but brief because there was no time to catch up. I slept at his place in Tiko. The following morning my friend Anyu came down to Tiko and we took off to Douala.

I thought that Anyu had money, but when we got to Douala, he made me understand that all the money he had on him was 50,000 francs. He didn't even have clothes or a decent pair of shoes. In his frustrations, he left behind the remainder of what was left of his belongings for the demanding siblings. He had sold most of what he had to raise the 50,000 francs. So he started spending that money in Douala. Then transport as well, he had to use some of that money to pay for his transportation. But, all the same, we left. We had planned to travel together, and it would have been difficult to suddenly turn around and tell him I didn't want his company anymore because he didn't have enough money. In Douala we took a bus to Yaoundé That day, if I am not mistaken, was the 4th of March 1994. That's the day that we set out for this journey to South Africa. In Yaoundé we had to take the train to Bertoua. It was my first time on a train. It wasn't decent, it wasn't decent at all. The train was overloaded and the seats were rusty.

From Bertoua, we took a Saviem bus to Batouri, and from there we got another bus for Berbérati. As we moved from town to town, and the mode of transportation was increasing from bad to worse. Driving along that road especially during the night is very risky. Drivers have to constantly be on the lookout for heavy trucks transporting timber. It is at night on such roads that one realizes the full extent to which Africa is being exploited. The kind of wood that leaves Cameroon for Europe is mind boggling. Little wonder that Cameroonians don't have jobs. How can they have jobs when everything is being exported unprocessed and untransformed as if all Cameroon has to offer are raw materials?

Berbérati is the border town between Cameroon and the Central African Republic. It was the first town in the latter country. In Berbérati, it was really easy with the customs and the immigration police. I learnt that as a Cameroonian crossing the border into Central Africa, one is treated with a lot of respect. As I progressed into Central Africa I discovered that that country actually relies on Cameroon. They import almost everything from Cameroon, right down to matches for lighting fires. Soap and salt are all imported from Cameroon. The only thing that they have in Central Africa is cassava and *nkum nkum* – cassava flour – which they export to Cameroon. They also have a lot of meat – bush meat mostly –, and maybe timber and their timber must go to Cameroon for it to be exported abroad because they are a landlocked country. I have always known Cameroon to be a dependent republic in terms of imports from France, Europe and even neighbouring Nigeria. This was the first time I witnessed Cameroon's relationships with other countries. I came to understand that there is more to the country's existence than dependency on its neighbours.

We slept in a small hotel in Berbérati. Berbérati is supposed to be the economic capital of Central African Republic, but it does not look any more developed than my home village. I could compare Berbérati to Santa, and Santa would beat it hands down, although Santa hardly begins to look like a serious town. And Bangui, the political capital, is more or less like Ndop, maybe Kumbo, but not a lot bigger. That's how developed Bangui is. Even the road leading to the presidency was only partly tarred and in patches. There were a lot of pot holes, and there was a lot of dust as well. We drove past in a taxi and someone showed me the presidency of the republic. There was nothing striking about it. It was like the house of someone ordinary. Not far from the road. Just there in its ordinary-ness. The thing that made it different was that there were soldiers and police guarding it. That's all. The country is not so rich., Although I have heard that it has lots of diamonds and gold, there was no sign of diamonds and gold in what I saw. Yet, Jean Bedel Bokassa must have seen something glorious to ordain himself emperor of the country! As someone from Cameroon, where we are used to saying we have nothing, all you need do is go to some of those countries, and you start feeling that Cameroon is better. Cameroon is better than most of these other countries.

There was one Saviem bus a day between Berbérati to Bangui. If you arrived in Berbérati after that one bus had left for Bangui, you would have to sleep over and get the next one the next day. I couldn't believe that there was only one bus between the economic capital and the political capital. It left at 9 o'clock in the morning. We caught the bus on time, got to Bangui, and lodged at a small rest house. We knew no one there and we couldn't afford expensive accommodation, so we asked for a very cheap place. At the rest house where we were lodging, we met another Cameroonian who used to trade between Bangui and Douala. He used to buy *nkum-nkum* and crayfish and sell them back in Cameroon, and he was making quite some money from what he told us about that trade. When this trader heard that we were going to South Africa he decided that he was going to come with us. There and then! He didn't plan to but just seeing us going to South Africa he decided that he was going to come with us. I don't know what happened, he tried, but once we had crossed over to Zaire he changed his mind and turned back. There are some people who don't know what they want.

The striking thing about staying in Bangui was the respect that the indigenes gave Cameroonians. My French is not good, and it was never good. My friend Anyu didn't speak French, and in Central Africa, the only language of communication was French and the indigenes themselves don't know French. When I was speaking my French, they thought I was from France. And for the three or four days that we were in that lodge the ladies around the vicinity used to come in the evening. They would come to the foyer of that lodge where we always sat and relaxed, seeking our attention. They would come just to sit and watch us and listen to us talk French. That was in the capital city of Central Africa. It was quite interesting. There, the thinking is that if you come from Cameroon you are closer to the white, to the Frenchman, so they must treat you differently.

We crossed into Zaire, Democratic Republic of Congo today. At the border town, at the immigration office, we were given visas into the country for three months. We paid quite some money. I can't remember how much now, but it must have been between 10 and 20 thousand francs. That is where it became more difficult, travelling the onward journey from there. When you go into Zaire you see the difference. In Central African Republic the interaction of the people there was very warm, welcoming, and respectful, but in Zaire you see the hostility from people beginning with the immigration officers, the police, and the army. Anyone in uniform wanted to pass for an immigration officer. Whether it was the police or the army, they would ask you for documents and evidence of your right of stay in the country. They would ask you for these documents, and whether or not you had them, they would ask you for money! Woe betides you if your documentation was not in order – worse still, if you hadn't documents at all. It was terrible!

It was so difficult travelling from that border village that we had to use big trucks carrying coffee to hide away from the pestering hostility of people in uniform. Those trucks transport coffee and other cash crops. At one point we had to climb on those trucks and sleep on the bags of coffee to be transported, and where their journey ended we had to sleep the night and think of other options to continue the journey. In some instances, we had to beg and plead for favours. How far we went on our journey depended on the trucks we could find and how far they were willing to go. At one point we took a truck, got to one village where its journey ended, and we had to end there as well. We stayed there for days. We didn't have a place to sleep, so we went into one of the bushes, and hurriedly put together a small hut of tree branches and grass. That was where we slept at night. After about a week, we gave up on hoping for a miraculous truck to appear and continued our journey on foot. It took us many days to get to a place that remotely resembled a town. It turned out that this was the town where Mobutu Sese Seko, who was the President of Zaire at the time, was born. It was just like Mvomeka in Sangmalema, where our own President, Popol, was born. While Mvomeka has sucked in resources in the manner an inlet lake sucks in water, Mobutu's home village did not seem to have attracted the attention of their foremost son. Was he ashamed of being identified with it or what? It was a miserable abandoned place, a ghost town, if town it was. The name of the town was Lisala, situated in the Equateur Province. Instead of making something of his place of birth, Mobutu developed the town of Gbadolite, which was thoroughly and jealously destroyed during the rebellion war by Jean-Pierre Bemba's *Mouvement de Libéation du Congo* (MLC).

So we got to Lisala. We located a small lodge, where we then slept. The only way forward was by boat on the River Congo. The last town before you cross into Rwanda is called Kissangani. It is a very big town. The boat leaves from Kissangani. It takes about a week to get to Mbandaka, the capital city of Equateur Province. Then it anchors at Mbandaka, then at Lisala and other ports, for people to load. And what are they loading on the boat? They load coffee, they load cash crops, and they load people as well. Most people here are not going anywhere in particular. They wanted to stay on the boat, just for the pleasure of it, at least so we thought. They paid their fare, they got into the boat and located their own small corner where they placed their mattresses, like an open bed, to sleep.

It was the rainy season in Zaire at that time of the year, just as was in Cameroon. As the journey unfolded, I realized the people did not board the boat just for the pleasure of it. The boat was a whole community of transactions of various kinds. When the people got into the boat, they started trading. Every time the boat made its stops along the River Congo to pick and drop passengers there was an opportunity for those on board to trade. It was a mobile market. The traders among those who boarded the boat with us bought fish from fishermen along the River Congo, from both sides of the river – the one side was Zaire and the other side was Congo Brazzaville – which they in turn sold to others on the boat. They would descale the fish, salt and smoke it and sell to customers on the boat, and along the way. The unsold fish amassed and smoked during the course of the journey was finally sold off in Kinshasa, where the traders would reinvest their money in buying consumer items to sell on the onward journey back to Kissangani. Before the boat left Kinshasa, they bought sugar, matches and other items to sell, and by the time they got to Kissangani they had bought and dried fish enough to sell there, and in turn buy other items to sell on their way back. It was like a circle of supply and demand that they had mastered. There are people for whom this is a way of life, from childhood to death. You find people who stay on the boat all their lives. You find people on that boat that will tell you everything about their journey. They will tell you they've been on this boat for ten years and many more. This was a strange thing that I discovered.

It wasn't easy for us to get onto the boat. I don't know exactly what they complained about, but they told us our passports did not permit us to board the boat. Some said we were Cameroonians and the boat was for Zaireans. We had to hire someone, a policeman, to take us in. He smuggled us in as if we needed a special visa to board the boat.

I had a small camera with me and I had learnt to use that camera in Zaire to save ourselves from harassment. Most of the places we passed in the course of our journey were backwards to our Cameroonian eye and experience. The people behaved as though they were in a pact with the devil – be it a police officer or a solider, all they wanted from you was money. For someone to tell you something in Zaire you needed to pay him or her. So I used that camera to fish us out of difficult situations. I was taking photos with the camera without any intention of printing them. But the whole idea was that most people tended to regard us as friends when we took photos with them. Photos were a big thing for them. To take someone's photo in those days was like a favour, it was like you were doing them a great favour. We always promised them that we're just going to the next town, we will print the photos there, and on our way back we will pass by and give them the photos. They were very excited. That's how they helped us without us paying. So we used that camera all along.

When we got onto the boat, the only space that was available for us to sit or lie down was next to a crocodile. This was a live crocodile that was tied with ropes and contained in a cage that was not solid enough. They used to feed the crocodile but only sparingly. And if it decided it needed an urgent meal, there was nowhere to run. We had no alternative but to make our beds next door to that crocodile. We felt like prey in the mouth of the crocodile. We had watched a film or two to know how violent the crocodile was when it was hungry. To say fright kept us on our toes is an understatement. But we had no choice.

That journey was to be from Mbandaka to Kinshasa. It was supposed to take two weeks, but at the end of the day it took us close to four weeks. The boat got grounded somewhere and we were on the same spot for one week. They had to send word – there was no instant communication like there is nowadays – to Kinshasa at snail speed. So we had to wait for another boat to come from Kinshasa, to which we were nearer, to take a message along to ask for another boat with a stronger engine to come and pull us out. Ours was a very big boat. During that week when we were stranded in the middle of nowhere, there was no food to eat. All of the foot was consumed on the boat.

Some fisherman took pity on us and took us in their boats to land surface, but that was in a bush, in a forest, with no villages in sight. We resorted to harvesting and eating wild leaves when our hunger became too much. We got so hungry that we used to harvest leaves and cook them. There was no salt, there was no seasoning, so we just boiled the leaves in dishes that we got from the boat, and we ate. My friend and I were hit particularly hard because we were the least prepared for the journey. Others had come prepared with their mattresses, blankets and bedding. They also had their stoves and everything they needed for the journey. But us, we hadn't known what to expect, so we had only our small bags with us. We had nothing to eat or to protect ourselves from the cold at night. It was quite difficult surviving that one week. We slept in the bush, in the forest and we just ate wild fruit and leaves.

Finally they came and pulled the boat out and we got to Kinshasa. In the course of the journey, we became friendly with one of the traders. He was on the boat with his wife. He was so friendly and he offered to help us, him and his wife. When things were fine and we were not yet stuck and reduced to eating leaves, he's the one who used to give us food during the journey. We didn't have much money, and even the little that we did have was not in the local currency. We had CFA. So this guy used to take CFA from us and give us Zaire, with which we were able to buy food to give to the wife to cook for us. That's how we survived that distance. This guy was so good to us. At least, so it appeared. We trusted him a lot. When we got to Kinshasa, we didn't know anybody. We didn't know how to go anywhere. This was the only person that we trusted to lead us out of the port. In Zaire, locals can immediately tell that you are a foreigner, especially when you talk. Even from your dress code they know and they always want to exploit you.

I had in my bag some wrapper material manufactured in Cameroon by CICAM. Prior to travelling out, I had done some homework, and was reliably informed that if I bought that material from Cameroon, I could sell it in Zaire and make a lot of money. So, when we were in Douala, I had bought a couple of pieces of that cloth and put it in my briefcase, before we took off. It was the same guy who was so friendly and who had offered to help us find our way in Kinshasa who then betrayed us. He must have thought we had lots of money or some precious metal or whatever that could make him an instant millionaire. We only discovered afterwards that he was a wolf in sheepskin. We would have gone out of the port without a problem. He pretended to help us but then suddenly disappeared when some soldiers or policemen spotted us and started coming in our direction. They arrested us and threw us into the cell and beat us.

I received beatings from soldiers in Zaire and they took my briefcase, after compelling me to open it. They took out all of the wrapper material, and they took all the money that we had as well. At one point I had, instinctively, separated the money I had and asked my friend to keep part of the money on him and I kept part. So when they took all the money I had in my briefcase, we were left with less than 50,000 francs.

After the police had beaten us badly and locked us up in a cell and taken the wrappers and money, the same friendly guy who had disappeared all of a sudden reappeared and pretended to plead for our freedom. It was afterwards that I started asking how he knew where we were. He came and took us out and said he was going to help us, to lodge us in his house until we found a way to go. When we got home, the very same day, he asked us to give him money to go and buy food to come and cook. He knew that they had robbed us, that they had taken our money. I was bleeding. His was a one room house. There was a bed for him and the wife, and there was a small mattress there for the kids too. He had two kids. The kids had to move to the big bed so that we could sleep on that mattress in the same room as the guy and his wife.

We stayed with this guy for close to five days and he finished our money. We discovered that this guy was not out to help us, he was out to exploit us and take all the money that we had. When the money had run out he threw us out of the house. He started telling us that he knew somewhere where there were Cameroonians. He said he could take us there and they would help us. That was after he had finished our money and knew that we were now a burden to him. We had no choice but to accept his offer. We took our bags, the few things that we had left, and followed him first to the Cameroon embassy where we insisted he took us. Only when there was no one there to help us, or rather, no one interested in helping us, did we go along with him to a certain place called Mosque D' Esouke. So we had to go with this guy to the mosque, where he told us that there are many Cameroonians who worshipped. There, we asked the Imam to let us sleep in the mosque. There were a couple of Cameroonians there. Papa Mohamed was one of them. Papa Isa was another. These old men had no convenient place to accommodate us. They were staying in their tiny shops with their families. We spent a couple of days in the mosque, sleeping in the mosque, no blanket, nothing, just sleeping on the carpet, and the mosquitoes were always there. It was a mosquito infested mosque, especially at night.

After a couple of days of sleeping in the mosque, God sent someone to help us.

Eventually, someone helped us, and I still remember this person, even today. Alhaji Ismail Kamgou was his name. He was a Cameroonian from the Western Province. He came and took us to his house. He had a big house. He gave us accommodation, food, and he even promised to help us to get our visas and pay our flights to South Africa. He was an elite among Cameroonians. Among Cameroonians in Kinshasa, he was considered rich. He was a Muslim, he was an Alhaji. He was also a marabout. I don't know how effective that was. Maybe that's where we learned one or two tricks, because later on in the journey we became marabouts as well.

We were excited with his promise to facilitate our journey to South Africa. But things are easier said than done. We spent one full year in Kinshasa in Kamgou's house. From the time that we arrived in Kinshasa to the time that we left, twelve months passed. It took us virtually a month to get from Cameroon to Kinshasa, and then we spent twelve months in Kinshasa. There was no doubting Kamgou's intention to help, but he needed the money to do so. He was a marabout, and depended on people coming and giving him money. So anytime that he planned to get money for us, the deal would not fall through. There was a South African embassy in Kinshasa at the time. In Cameroon and most central African countries, everyone seeking a South African visa had to travel to Kinshasa, in those days.

One of the disagreeable experiences of our stay in Papa Alhaji's house – that's how we used to call it: Papa Alhaji's house – was his wife. Papa Alhaji was extremely good, very accommodating, very friendly, helpful and respectful. But his wife, who was from Zaire, was very unlike him. It would appear that she came from a not so well-to-do family and that her parents were in that same town. In exchange for treating people, Papa Alhaji used to ask people to pay him in food, not so much in money. Then he used to convert that food into money when he needed it. Someone would bring like ten bags of rice, ten bags of salt, a goat and things like that. So there used to be a lot of food at home – fish, oil, rice, all of the nice things. These were extreme rarities in the average Zairean household, even in Kinshasa, the capital. His wife used to steal the food and take it to the family most of the time. She was very greedy, indeed, so much so that she could only give us food when Papa Alhaji was there. The house used to team with visitors, most of them hungry people, hoping to get a decent meal. But that was only possible when Papa Alhaji was at home. If he was not there, we could not eat at home. The woman was not kind to us or to anyone else who came to eat her food. It wasn't as if food was lacking. When she cooked and if Papa Alhaji was not at home, we did not eat.

It wasn't easy as we had no money. Then finally we asked ourselves what in effect we were doing there. What were we going to do? Wasn't it self-defeating for us to continue waiting for Papa Alhaji to treat people and for them to give him money? What must we do? We embarked on a begging spree. I was a Muslim then from Saudi Arabia, my friend was not a Muslim, but now that we were accommodated by a Muslim, my friend got converted into Islam. Now we were both Muslims. The Muslim fraternity is so close and so helpful when you're in need. My friend initiated an idea that we should go to different mosques and write a letter to the Imam that they should raise funds for us, for this and that. There is what they call Zarka. You come and stand and hold out your plate and people come and put money inside for you. So we used to do that – begging.

There was another Alhaji, a Nigerian who used to go to

Nigeria to import things into Zaire and sell and supply to shops. One of the things that he used to import was posters – of musicians and pop stars mostly, Bob Marley, Madonna and so on. So we went to him to negotiate to sell his posters for a commission. That's where I started the kind of business that I am doing now. That's where I got the inspiration. Oh no, actually I used to market laboratory reagents from Nigeria, and jewellery and clothing from Saudi Arabia. I also used to buy sugarcane, pineapples, palm oil etc. from Bali and Ashong to sell in the Ndapang Market in Pinyin. I guess I was born with the business instinct, or got it by inheritance. So we would collect posters from this other Alhaji, go and sell and bring back his money and keep our commission. We raised quite a lot of money that way. Posters in Zaire at that time were moving – everyone wanted them. They were particularly sought after by poor people. You go into someone's house, there is nothing else, almost no furniture or utensil, but on the wall you find a larger than life poster of Bob Marley, Michel Sardou, Joe Dassin, Jonny Halliday, Claude François or another superstar, male and female alike. We started selling those posters, hawking on the streets, but not for long because it landed me in jail again.

There were pornographic posters that used to make us a lot more money. There was a certain busy place where when I hawked and I was tired, I would go there and just display my posters for people to come and buy. Then one of those days I displayed my posters and a policeman came and told me that he wanted one of those pornographic posters. He was not formerly dressed as a policeman. He came disguised. Then I gave it to him. He just called his colleagues and they came and arrested me, took all my posters, took me to the police cell and locked me up. I was in the cell for five days and no one knew where I was. My friend and Papa Alhaji were looking for me all over Kinshasa until someone who was in the cell as well was released and I sent him to go to that address with a message. That's how Papa Alhaji came to release me. I lost all those posters, the money that I sold for that day, they took everything. That was the second time I was jailed in Zaire. It was not a good thing. If we say the uniformed officers in Cameroon are brutal, Zaire is worse. But what could we do? We went back to work. I had to pay off the things that were stolen and we started doing it again.

One of the highlights of us staying in that place was that we actually appeared on TV. Our host was a very strong man. There was a talk show about traditional medicine, so our host took us there and we were in the panel, not active but just there. In the evening news they showed us. My friend and I were there with him. That was a good thing. That was one of the things that made me smile. But the rest of my experience was one bitter encounter after another. To date, when you meet a *Zairois* – as Zaireans were called in French – for the first time, the first thing that he'll tell you is 'be careful with my brothers, they are dangerous'. They seem to be the good guys warning you that their brothers are going to dupe you, only for them to turn out being the ones who dupe you. All of them, that's how they are. Actually, in Congo Brazzaville there's a saying that if you see a *Zairois* and a snake, let the snake go, kill the *Zairois* first. That's how bad they are. It is the same saying we have in Cameroon about the French, that if you see a Frenchman and a snake, kill the Frenchman and leave the snake.

There was this guy who posed as someone who wanted to help us in a way, because he took us around town but at the end of the day he too was a true *Zairois*. We also became an unofficial consultant among youths on how to travel to Cameroon. *Zairois* love travelling to Cameroon, and most of their artists travelling to Europe want to go through Cameroon. They will come to Cameron and open barbing saloons and things like that and they make money and they go to France or to Belgium. What they teach us is that you can make money anywhere. It's your mentality that matters.

There is the story of a Ghanaian who came to Cameroon and he was accommodated by my friend Anyu. They gave him an empty room in a *karabot* house in Victoria. He was going around fixing shoes, one of those shoe menders Cameroonians generally refer to by the sound they make to attract your attention – *kok-kok*. In his room there was nothing, it was just a mat and a blanket. Every morning he would get up, and go *kok-koking* from door to door to fix shoes. And they thought that this guy was uneducated, they thought he had nothing. People were having pity on this guy, and they thought he was a beggar. But this guy stayed in my friend's house for two years quietly going about the business of door to door shoe repairing. One morning they checked and the Ghanaian was not there. He had disappeared. After two weeks he called from Japan to apologize for leaving without telling anyone. During his two years in Cameroon, he had a goal to achieve and he achieved it. He was there to save money enough to take him to Japan, and it didn't matter that he was a degree holder. The serious people in life are not those who sound like empty calabashes. Put yourself low and achieve mountains. Let the winds of your achievements blow your trumpet.

In the business of making money, it doesn't matter where you go. It's just your mentality. I say this is because most of the *Zairois* who come to Cameroon are successful. It's the way that they think, they think that Cameroon is like their Eden and when they come there, there will be lots of opportunities. If you look for opportunities you'll see them. What they look for is the odd jobs. The same is true of most Africans who came to

South Africa. They become rich not because of anything else but because they see opportunities that South Africans don't see, like what we were doing in Zaire, selling posters. *Zairois* were so poor. Most of them had been devastated for decades by the sterile regime of Mobutu Sese Seko. But they would not do what we were doing; they would not go about hawking. They would not do it. Their citizenship was perhaps too precious in their eyes for them to soil with seeking to make ends meet by hawking. Maybe one needs to go away from home – like a prophet who is never respected in his homeland – to seek success where one has nothing to lose – not even the privilege of second or third class citizenship.

After trying to raise money, we started looking for a way out, how to travel. So we decided we were going to go through Angola. It is easy sitting in your room and planning an itinerary using a map in some book, and reading about a place you know nothing about or how to get there. That is what I did before we set out on this journey. But as we progressed, the reality set in and things changed in so many ways. We had to go and get a visa, so we went to the Angolan embassy in Kinshasa. We got the visa. We had some friends too who helped us, thanks to Papa Alhaji. But before that, in our efforts to raise money, we went to the Cameroon embassy again to find out if they could help us in any way. So they told us they could help us by putting us on the plane on Cameroon Airlines back to Douala. It was really tough on us and we were tempted to say yes. It was the only help they could give us. They couldn't help us with money for food, they couldn't help us with anything else but they could put us on the plane to Douala.

We accepted. Our calculation was that once they gave us the air tickets we could exchange them for cash. Someone had told us that it was possible to exchange tickets for money in that way. But the day that they were supposed to give us the air tickets, we went to the embassy and they told us that they will not give us tickets. They told us to come to the embassy on the morning of the appointment day, and they will drive us to the airport and put us on the plane and give us the tickets there at the airport. So we said ok, left and never went back. On that day we didn't go. That was not the sort of help we needed. We wanted an onward and not backward journey. I didn't see myself going back to Cameroon because I had nothing to show for my troubles. I resisted Anyu's insinuations and temptations of going back. To me, it had to be that we moved forward, and never backwards, no matter the circumstances.

With some help from others we got a visa to go to Angola and we raised money that we thought was enough to take us, maybe to South Africa. If I am not mistaken we had just over 500 American dollars. Around that! Once we got the visas in our passports we decided to start off for Luanda. But first, we had to go through Cabinda, the Angolan island town between Congo Brazzaville, Zaire and mainland Angola. We had to travel from Kinshasa to a place called Matadi, a port city. It is supposed to be the economic capital of Zaire. And the way they promoted Matadi to us, it was like we are going to a very big city. This was a journey of about 60km between Kinshasa and Matadi, but it took us three days by truck. When we finally got there, this place was like another Santa. Unlike Kinshasa, which resembled a city in those days even though most of the buildings and roads were dilapidated, Matadi and other cities in Zaire were nothing to write home about, though this country is known as one of the richest in Africa in terms of minerals. Travelling in Zaire was a nightmare due to the lack of roads or failure to maintain those dug by the Belgians, the colonial masters before independence. We got to Matadi, and we slept there somewhere. When we went to the border to cross into Cabinda with the visas we had been issued they told us that the visas were fake. They said we were not supposed to enter Cabinda, that Cabinda needed a special visa. We never had that visa. Ah! That journey was tough. Then they repatriated us back to Matadi. Then we had to smuggle ourselves back into Cabinda by jumping over border fences, and it was once again like the experience of Jeddah in Saudi Arabia that I had to jump borders. But it was not as difficult. We hired someone to take us across so we smuggled ourselves into Cabinda. When we got to Cabinda they caught us again, but this time they didn't deport us, they locked us up. But fortunately enough we'd left Zaire, we were in Angola, and that's what mattered.

I think we were in jail for close to a week and there's always a good Samaritan. One good Samaritan came to our aid. We somehow knew this guy from Zaire. We never knew him well facially or physically but we were told that he was always there, he was a Muslim. It was a chance meeting. He came to see someone who was jailed, and we met him. He bailed us out. I don't know how he did it but he took us out, and gave us accommodation in the mosque. We were there for a few days trying to find a way to get to Luanda, the capital city. The only way to get there was by air, because there were no good roads. Cabinda is an island. If you have to go by road, you still have to go by sea to get to Angola mainland and that would take weeks, because the roads were bad and at that time it was also dangerous. Jonas Savimbi and his rebel group infested Angola at that time. So it was not safe travelling by road. It was either by air or nothing. This was where I actually realized that you can smuggle yourself into the plane. In Angola, even right there in Cabinda, if you cannot speak Portuguese it's already a crime. It's just like in Zaire, Kinshasa, if you cannot speak Lingala, it's a crime. They rough-handle you immediately when they know that you're not one of them, and not being one of them is a crime to them. You're not welcomed to the country. Angola was very hostile at the time, right down to the average Angolan, very hostile.

Cabinda is a very rich island. It's like a state inside Angola, and there's a lot of oil there. But the people in Cabinda, the indigenes of Cabinda have got their own grudges against the government, which they blame for extracting their riches and failing to develop the place. It's a very small place but not developed, despite the wealth of oil they smear their country with. They detest the insensitivity of the Angolan government which extracts all their oil and uses it for other things and for war, but not for development. The people are so disgruntled they were fighting for their independence, and they vent it out on foreigners as well. So it was going to be difficult for us to get onto the plane, because we had to speak. We had to at least say something somewhere, but we could not speak Portuguese. They were bound to find out that we were not from Angola.

We hired someone, an army officer, to smuggle us into the plane. In these countries, the dollar can buy anything and anyone. It took us longer. I can't remember how much longer. There was a plane from Cabinda to Luanda either once a week or two times a week. The first time we tried we didn't succeed, so we had to wait again for another week. I think we waited for another three or four days. Finally the army officer smuggled us into the plane, which was full, overloaded. We had no seats. It was my first experience seeing that you can enter a plane and sit on the floor. Back home, just going into the plane gave you a good feeling that you're entering a plane. This was most certainly something new – to enter a plane and sit on the floor of the plane as an overload passenger! There were some people who were standing, making use of some of the seats as support so that they shouldn't fall. When the plane was turning, they would fall on us. It was chaos in the plane. But then, we finally got to Luanda, leaving the nightmare of Cabinda behind us.

The next nightmare was how to get out of the airport in Luanda. We knew no one, we didn't know how we were going to do it but the man who bailed us out in Cabinda had directed us on what to do once we were out of the airport. He indicated that once we got out of the airport, we would find lots of West Africans, Somalis and many other non-Angolans. We should ask for the mosque, and seek shelter there. First, we had to get out of the airport. On our way out after landing in Luanda, my friend was apprehended. I pretended as if I didn't know him and I left. I don't know how I passed the security and the immigration police. I just walked out of the arrivals hall. I saw a man. He was standing by a car. I approached him, asked him if he knew that mosque, and he said yes! I asked him if there was a contact person for the mosque. He said yes. Then I informed him that there were two of us, but that my friend had been taken hostage by the police. Could he do something? He said ok. He went in and I don't know how he managed it but he came back with my friend.

The man was very honest. He was quite unlike others in Zaire where they always duped us. He took his own money and bribed the policeman who had detained my friend, and then he told us the exact amount. We paid him back. It was a bit strange. If this man had been a *Zairois*, he would most probably have taken everything from us and would have ensured that we were arrested and jailed. But this man was not like that. Perhaps other *Zairois* are not like that too, but everyone we encountered certainly was. We could say we had met some honest people along the way though. This man drove us to the mosque where we were supposed to lodge. It was a small mosque with a big yard and another small house where stranded people could sleep on a mat on the floor. That's where we lodged and we stayed in Luanda for three weeks. When I left Cameroon, we spent twelve months in Kinshasa, and before we got to Kinshasa we had spent like one month on the way. Cabinda, I think it was about two weeks or so, Luanda about three weeks. It had been about fourteen months now - we desperately sought South Africa.

The experience that we had in Luanda was almost the same as we had had in Zaire in the sense that our money dried up. But unlike in Zaire where we were robbed of our money, in Luanda our money disappeared when we left Kinshasa. We had about $500, which we thought was a lot of money to take us to South Africa. But the bribes we had to pay ate rapidly into our money. We were staying at the mosque and we went through some very disturbing experiences in Luanda.

With our money finished, we had to look for money. We spoke neither Portuguese nor any of the local languages of Luanda. Yet we needed money. We needed money and we needed a visa to enter Namibia, our next stop. It was time for us to practice what we had learnt in Zaire from Papa Alhaji, the marabout with whom we stayed. We used to observe him at work, and had accompanied him to TV on a public debate on traditional medicine. So we knew a thing or two about his art of fortune telling and diviner prowess. It was time to summon that knowledge for survival's sake.

We discovered that in Luanda, the indigenes liked black medicine a lot. We decided to become marabouts. My friend Anyu was very good with that, because he had a traditional doctor in Cameroon who was his friend. I was the anchor-man. I had to go out and look for customers. My friend would sit at the Mosque, clandestinely, and customers would come and meet him for consultations. He demanded a lot of things from them. When these traditional doctors say that they do things, it's a lie! A big lie! Some, maybe, but a majority of them out there are just out to take your money. What we did was this: I would go out and with the bit of French I knew, even though my French was not good, we tried to communicate. I had an Angolan acquaintance who could speak French, so we were communicating in French. We would go out, enter a drinking spot, then we would sit next to someone, then I would tell him in French what to do. I would ask him to listen to what people in the bar were saying, and find out a thing or two about those present, especially the ones we were targeting. There were some people at bar at a particular time who you would meet, and then the next day, at the same time, they would be there again. It was always good to go and observe them. We tried to learn something about each person. My informant would narrate to me whatever he had learned about the person we were targeting – his name, where he came from, etc. Sometimes the informant would actually go up to that person and make him a friend, with the intention of gathering as much information as possible about them, their origins, their life and their circumstances. We were particularly interested in finding out as much as we could beforehand about the problems people were facing. Once my informant had given me all the details and background information I needed, I would then approach the person with the confidence of a diviner, knowing that the person would be impressed by my magical and mystical knowledge of them and their inner truths. When I had convinced him that he needed a cure from his afflictions, we would then take him to my friend the marabout.

By the time the target went to my friend, all his details were available to him. As soon as the target walked in, my friend would shout his name, making the target conclude that the diviner must be good since he knew his name. Imagine that you walk into a native doctor's place and he calls your name, you don't know him, he doesn't know you. That alone was a big sign that the native doctor must be really good. Things will only get better as the doctor begins to tell him everything about him, pretending that the information was being revealed by the cowries he threw. Whenever my friend threw cowries, he would tell the person their name, where they came from, what their job was, as well as the problems that worried them. Since my friend did not speak Portuguese or any of the local languages, everything he said had to be translated by the local assistant we used. When he had convinced the person consulting him, my friend would then state that he could solve all their problems for a fee, and consulting his cowries, he would say the ancestors needed two he-goats, three bags of rice, and a certain amount in the local Angolan currency.

That's how we got money. Before we knew it we got so many bags of rice, goats, fish oil, and groundnut oil. That's what our boss used to ask in Zaire, so we asked for the same things and converted that into money, sold them and made money, that's how we made money. When we thought that we had enough money, we had to leave. The problem now was that our visas had expired. Not really expired as such, but we did not have an entry into Angola, so how were we to get out of a country when there was no record that we had entered? They would not give us a visa to go to Namibia. There was no entry stamped on our passports and there was no authentic visa.

We found a way. We found someone to go to the airport and stamp the entry on our passports. Then we became regular. We went to the Namibian consulate and they told us they could not give us a visa to go to Namibia because we didn't have a return ticket and we didn't have enough money to show. We kept on going there every single day in the hope that they might change their minds and issue us with visas. When we kept going, the person who was attending to us went and reported us, and asked the security not to let us in again. The ambassador of Namibia to Angola was a woman. I know that women have soft hearts, so one day I went to the embassy and waited for her to arrive at the office. I had studied her arrival times. I positioned myself somewhere near the gate, ready to come out once the security had opened the gate for her. So she came and they were opening the gate and I stood in front of the car. The security guards almost killed me! I insisted I needed to speak with the ambassador. There was nothing she could do but listen to me. She said they must let me speak.

So I forced myself on the ambassador. She had to see me. She took me and my friend into her office and we presented our case. My passport had as profession, lawyer, my friend had the same profession too. We had made our findings and discovered that there was a conference that was supposed to be held in Windhoek, Namibia and it was something to do with human rights. So we told this woman that we were from Cameroon, and that we worked for a certain human rights group. Why we didn't have our credentials was because we were robbed and hence were obliged to travel through the convoluted manner in which we found ourselves. We had to attend that conference in Windhoek. We convinced the woman! She granted us the visas and ordered that the visas be given to us. That was the solution to that problem.

What I did, I had done so many times when I was faced with a situation. In African countries when you want to get something done you go to the boss. Even here in South Africa, when you go somewhere and you try to get something they will always block you, and block you and block you, but when you go to the person who is in charge, there is no problem. I've seen that in many cases getting a problem solved is a problem, and getting to the person who is in charge is equally a problem, but once you are able to access that person your problem is solved. That's exactly what happened to us because this woman was so good, very receptive, and very sympathetic. While all those intermediary staff were giving us trouble along the way, the issue was a simple one.

We left Luanda with some sad memories. One of them was the feast of the ram. It was Ramadan day. We were sitting inside the mosque where we were staying. They brought us food. Being Ramadan, Muslims always eat together. There was a bowl of rice that we were eating. We ate with the hands as we were used to. The guy who used to help us a lot – Yusuf was his name – was with us, eating with us. Someone opened the gate and called "Yusuf! Yusuf come!" Yusuf went. He was sitting next to me. He left the rice and went out. In a few minutes, we heard a gunshot and people started screaming. When we went out we saw Yusuf lying in a pool of blood, dead, just like that. That's how dangerous it was in Angola at the time.

Along the road one day – it was a busy road – someone passed me. This guy walked past and our bodies touched each other, because it was crowded. He didn't go one step away from me. I heard a gunshot and the guy was on the floor, right next to me. Probably if I was not lucky, I would have had blood on my clothes. He was dead. Angola was dangerous at the time. People used guns at will, they just shot and killed and went free. Nobody went after them or did anything. There was no police protection, nothing. It was like a jungle.

There was a certain Freedom Park, a place where all the war victims who were helpless went to beg. If you went to that place, you came face to face with war as a bad thing. War was still raging on in Angola at that time. This was 1995. Savimbi was still very active and there were rebel groups, here and there, killing people. I went to that park and I saw what war can do to people. There were thousands and thousands of people with no legs, some with no arms, some with a half nose or mouth, no ear, and deformed heads. It was like a zoo, a zoo for deformed humans. It's really bad. War is not a good thing!

War can do things to people. In Luanda at the time you could see that this was once a wonderful city, full of skyscrapers and very good buildings in those days. They were abandoned because of the war. Every now and again we spotted very nice buildings riddled with holes from bullets. We went to Angola at a time when the war was still very bad. One of the reasons why travelling in overcrowded planes seemed so normal and desired was because it was dangerous travelling by land. There were rebel road blocks everywhere on the main roads, with rebels ready to kill everyone in the car. So the government had made flying cheaper than driving. In Angola, to travel by air is like travelling by land here in South Africa. It is not expensive. All citizens can afford a flight. That was the government's bid to make it easy for them to travel. That's why the planes were overloaded. They were buses in the air.

That's Angola. Luanda was such a beautiful city but because of the war, it was in very bad shape. It was dirty. Buildings were dilapidated, gunned down by soldiers. The people that we meet at Freedom Park gave me sleepless nights. I had nightmares. I still do. Sometimes I would wake up with a start, asking myself why I left Cameroon. Was it worth it? Just imagine. Someone is sitting with you, they call him out and he's dead. It could be you. Someone is passing by you and they shoot them dead. What if that bullet was not meant for that person? What if it was actually meant for me? It could have been some crazy idiot who just wanted to shoot! God guided us. God was in control.

The incidents of gunshots in Luanda reminded me of a similar incident in Cameroon, when the Social Democratic Front party was launched in Abakwa in 1992. I remember the crowd marching to the governor's office, when gendarmes and police and the army were dispatched to shoot and kill. These men of force in uniform came in their Land Rovers and army trucks. Ordinarily, they should have used rubber bullets and water cannons, had their sole brief been to achieve crowd control. But they had been instructed to shoot to kill, by a trigger-happy state rattled by the prospect of real and transparent multiparty democracy.

There was no one on the streets except those of us who were marching. A roving car with gendarmes and soldiers was passing, and when they saw us, they shot into us. There were about four of us standing there. I had my foot on the floor, the next guy stood next to me. They shot right under my foot and my shoe was torn by that bullet. It was not a rubber bullet because a rubber bullet cannot go into a wall. It tore my shoes and went into the ground, and I pushed this guy when I felt something. There was blood coming out. It was a reflex action. I pushed this guy and he fell. If I didn't push my friend, he would have been dead because it went into the ground, it went down and it came out where my friend was standing. It could have got him anywhere in the leg or stomach. Then we went into the house. I ran for my dear life, I got home and never went back. Six innocent people lost their lives that day, shot dead by soldiers, gendarmes and the police mobilized to ensure that democracy was not to be activated beyond lip service in our Autocratic Republic of Cameroon.

When I visited Cameroon recently, I saw one of the more fortunate victims of our march of defiance. He had lost his hands when he unwittingly picked up a hand grenade the soldiers had thrown into the crowd on that fateful day. I met him while I was taking the bus in Abakwa. He was begging, he was going from passenger to passenger begging with those stumps of arms. I had even forgotten about him and someone told me that was the guy whose hands were amputated because of the grenade. I asked myself, this guy was fighting a just cause at the time; he was fighting for the people. When he had his misfortune, what became of him? He's still begging, but some of the people that are at the helm of the party are enjoying themselves. They send their kids to fancy schools abroad, their spouses go on shopping sprees to Paris, London, Washington etc., and they go on holidays to the Bahamas, Barbados, and Mauritius Island.. It is the less fortunate that fight wars, it is they that fight for change, and that bring the fortunate to power. And when they get to power, they forget about those who got them there. I don't think it's right. I don't think it's right.

That's what happens with war. The weak and the innocents are the ones who suffer, because they have no one to talk for them. They have no one to defend them. They have no means of doing things for themselves. So they are the ones who suffer. This is the fate of those at Freedom Park. Those war victims in Luanda, the guys with the grenade arms, the ones who lost their lives in the struggle, and their families, those are the weak people, the poor ones. The leaders of all those factions that were fighting, the party leaders, they are sitting in their mansions, sitting on good chairs, eating good food, sleeping nightmare free sleep. But those who fight on the ground are those who are suffering. I don't think war is a good thing. Violence doesn't pay and somehow I feel that those who mastermind violence in war -in every case- do it for their own benefit. They do it for themselves, not for the people. I don't think that someone who really loves people would send them to war. I don't think so, because in the long run the people will suffer. The leaders are the ones enjoying it. I don't like war. Change can be achieved through peaceful means, nonviolence. Ask Mahatma Ghandi, Martin Luther King, Grandpa Tata Madiba Mandela, peace be upon them.

It was time to leave Angola. It was time to leave Luanda.

This time it was much easier to get into the plane. Maybe because when you move away from central Africa, you know you're moving into civilization. I don't know, but that's the way I saw it. The people on the plane that we took from Luanda to the village on the Namibian border the people were friendly and more of them could speak English. It was quite a different experience. It was not like in Cabinda. We had much easier access to the plane. We had seats on the plane, even though it was still overloaded. But a nightmare that I will never forget happened. Something happened to that plane. The weather was bad and there was no power in that airport where we were supposed to land. I think the pilots just piloted the plane because they knew where that airport was. There was no tower. They didn't communicate with anyone. Landing was pure guesswork. The weather was bad. It was windy and cloudy and the plane started going down like a stone.

The plane was taking a free fall. It was like the end of life for us. The problem wasn't fuel, it was just the weather and the pilot could not see. It went down and when he realized himself, we were on top of trees. We started cutting trees down, then it picked up again. The pilot was actually looking for that airport, he lost his balance, didn't find the airport and I was told that we went into Namibian territory. We were told afterwards that when it went into Namibian territory they threatened to shoot it down because it had no right to cross Namibian territory, so it found its way back and we kept on circling and circling until we landed. In that plane, when everyone thought it was the end, people who were smoking and drinking and abusing people and doing whatever, they started praying. They became very good Christians. People started praying in tongues.

I don't know what language I was using to pray. My friend was talking in a language that I did not understand. It was like chaos, it was like the tower of Babel. Everyone was speaking their own language. That was an experience. That experience taught me that at any time, even if you don't go to church, even if you're not a Christian, Muslim or believer of any kind, everyone knows that there's someone up there that they can always turn to when there's no one else to turn to. The way everyone was praying in that plane, was like everyone were staunch priests, including me. When you think it is the end, sometimes prayers can help. Prayers help – we survived, and we landed.

At the airport, there were two houses that were destroyed by guns, by war. There was no tower. The runway was like a small tarred road with pot-holes. I knew the police or army would still give us problems. So when people were standing on the line I went somewhere as if I was going to pee and I discovered there was a big hole at the back of the building, so I just went through the hole and I went out of the airport. My friend followed. We both came out of that airport, took a taxi to the border crossing.

The border village where we landed was not far from Namibia. It was another story, we checked out of the Angolan side. We still had to use tricks. I became a master of tricks. I remember a black South African. He was driving his own car into Angola and I heard him speaking English. So when people were in the queue I went up to him and greeted him and I made sure that all those policemen who were doing the controls saw me talking to this guy. I created a conversation. He told me he was going to Angola. He was always going there to do business, and then come back. I discovered that this guy was a big guy and they knew him because he was just ordering everyone around and I went up to him and greeted him. I said I knew him. I am always on this road. I've seen him so many times. He told me he was from South Africa, Johannesburg, precisely. The guy was so warm. Everyone saw me talking to him. So when I left, instead of standing on the queue, I just took my bag, called my friend, and said come let's go, you must hurry because this guy needs us. When we got there they just stamped our passports and we went in.

When we checked out of Angola, on entering Namibia, everything was cool until we went to immigration. The immigration police told us we could not enter. I had created a friendship with one guys who was Angolan, with the understanding that he would take us from that town and show us around. I told this guy to hold my bag, so he took my bag and I took his and we walked in. My friend was held back. We walked in and we started talking. The guy was known by those around. We were talking about human rights conferences which I was allegedly there to attend. All of them at the borders understand English, and were able to overhear us discussing our participation at the conference and our commitment to defending human rights. I went in now and I saw my friend and I asked the immigration officer who was detaining him what's wrong. Are you abusing his human rights again? The Angolan actually believed me, and introduced me to the immigration police as a human rights lawyer from Cameroon, adding that we were headed for Windhoek to attend the human rights conference. When they checked our passports, they confirmed that we were indeed lawyers. They stamped our passports and wished us well. I became the boss. I took my friend, that's how we entered Namibia.

From there we took a taxi to the nearest town with the help of that friend but when we got to that town, something again happened. In Angola it was hot, when you drink water you can see it is hot. My friend was thirsty. In that small border town, there was a tap out there. I asked my friend to go and drink. We had no money to buy water. Then Anyu went and opened that tap and drank. He ran back to me holding his mouth in an awkward manner, "You know we don reach for Whiteman kontri oh", he said. "We don reach for Whiteman kontri. Dis kontri bad, even pomp, dem di put water for fridge. Dis one na developed kontri." It was winter in Namibia, so the water was cold. But we didn't know that. So my friend actually convinced me that the water was coming from a fridge. They had to put water in a fridge for it to run in the tap and we drank that water. It was so nice. We saw apples. Since we came from Cameroon, it was the first place where we saw apples being sold on the streets. With the small money we had, we bought a lot of apples and started eating. It was like a full meal to us. We ate and felt good, different.

We entered Namibia and took a bus. We had to travel by night. It was not a big bus. It was like the taxis here in Cape Town. I think that border town was called Oshakati. We had to go from there down to Windhoek. It was winter. When we got to Windhoek it was night. The contact that we had in Windhoek was not a mosque, but a place for refugees, a place where they lodged stranded people. During our travels, all along we were being accommodated by Muslims. When we arrived in Windhoek the person who directed us did not know where this place was, and we could not go there at midnight either. He took us to his place. It was the first time I saw a shack, what they call here in South Africa a nkuku. A shack is like a very small house built with wood or zinc. It's like karabot in Cameroon. But a karabot is better, much better constructed than those shacks. That shack that this man called his house was like an open air dwelling in winter. The bitterly cold wind assaulted us at will. The shack was not protected at all, it was just pieces of plank wood put together with some cheap zinc on top, and that was the man's house. He was the driver of that combi. So he took us there and said we should go in and sleep. We went into that house. I've never slept in a shack before. I was not ready for that! I didn't know that there were shacks in a Whiteman's country, where water comes from the fridge for everyone to drink.

It was a surprise to me. We went into that place, his wife was there, and his kid was sleeping. In South Africa, I know most people who stay in shacks are either youngsters who want to be independent from their parents or migrants from the villages who come to work in the cities. But in Windhoek I didn't know what I know today, so I didn't find out if our host came from elsewhere or if that was really his home. I couldn't sleep in that shack. It just didn't feel right for me. I begged this guy to please let me sleep in the combi. He let me and my friend sleep in the combi. I had never experienced winter before then, and winter in Namibia was harsh at that time. I don't know if it's still harsh now but it was very, very harsh. At night it was so cold that I could not even open the door to go and pee. I had to pee in my clothes - I did this consciously and felt warmer when I did! I had to pee in my pants, knowingly; I was shaking; it was tough. Before I realized it I was peeing in my pant and it was nice and feeling good. It felt good doing it. I really felt good doing that because it was warm.

Finally, the dawn that we were waiting for arrived. It was a long night, those few hours. It was better when the combi was moving because the heater was on. At dawn we asked this man to take us to town and find that place where we were supposed to be lodged. He got us a taxi. It was a great help because, even though the taxi man didn't know the place, he went and looked for it and left us there. We got there and met the lady who was in charge. It was like a night shelter for the Muslims, for stranded Muslims, for travellers. We were well received. At least, life in that place was not as bad. They gave us food. The woman who was in charge was really receptive, friendly. We made friends there as well.

In Kinshasa we met a guy. His passport name was Eric. That's how people know him, even today. But that's not his real name. Eric met us in Kinshasa. When we were there we actually received a lot of other people. Eric was one of them. When he came, he posed as a Cameroonian, and he was travelling on a Cameroonian passport. When he got to Kinshasa we were glad to meet our brother. They brought him to us to help him as he was stranded as well. They brought him to us knowing that we were Cameroonians. But when I asked Eric, where do you come from? He said he came from Kombone Mission. I didn't know where Kombone Mission was situated in Cameroon at the time, so I assumed it did not exist. But it actually exists, Kombone, but apparently no Mission. It is a village in the Ndian Division of the South West Region. That aside, I later discovered that he was actually a Nigerian who apparently had a fake Cameroonian passport. The only place he knew in Cameroon was Kombone Mission, so everywhere he went he announced that he was from Kombone Mission. Eric was a very fast guy – super fast! We left him in Kinshasa and met him in Namibia. That's how fast he was.

Another person we met in Kinshasa was one francophone Cameroonian who was on an adventure. He said he wanted to go somewhere I cannot remember. Then when he got to Kinshasa he discovered that it was tough. So he wanted to go back home, but he wanted to take a boat and cross the River Congo, into Congo Brazzaville and continue his journey back to Cameroon. But he was robbed in the boat and thrown into the sea! We heard news that everything of his was taken and he was thrown into the sea by those greedy Zaireans, those armed robbers. It was terrible! We never knew where exactly in Cameroon he came from. We never knew whom to start contacting. That was the kind of case where someone goes missing, you don't know where he's gone to, after some time you'll just have to organize a funeral to mourn his death without a corpse. He was thrown into the river for sharks or crocodiles to feed on. That's how dangerous it is travelling. But one just can't fold one's arms and sit on one spot because the world out there is dangerous, can one?

In Windhoek there was another Cameroonian who we met, with his wife, Koposi. They were headed for South Africa as well. Several years ago today I gathered that she had died. She was then living and working in the Eastern Cape. The husband abandoned her in Cape Town and left. I don't know where he went to, probably Cameroon. Theirs was a marriage of convenience. Then we met two other guys, Mosi and Ango from Abakwa, who afterwards joined us in Cape Town. We hosted them for quite a while in our flat in Kensington. Mosi later travelled to the US where he said he had a job as an IT technician. Ango travelled to Sydney, Australia and much later, to the UK. I haven't heard of them since. They were working in a construction site in Windhoek when we met them. They had come in just like us, got stranded, and had to do odd jobs to raise money.

We were in Windhoek for about three weeks. In two weeks the money ran out. Each and every country we went to, we had to look for money. In Windhoek we didn't try practicing being marabouts or hawking as a solution to our financial problems. But what we did instead to raise money in Windhoek was we solicited for help from Muslim brothers who came to where we were staying. We raised some money. It wasn't much money that was needed to cross to South Africa.

We were surprised to find Eric from Kombone Mission in Windhoek. We didn't know he had left Kinshasa and settled in Namibia. We discovered as well that he had become what we Cameroonians normally refer to as a "docky man" or "docky doctor" – someone who solves all problems pertaining to various documents often required by officials to validate our existence or aspects thereof. He was issuing visas and all sorts of documents to people. That was his job. He was a document doctor, whom others consulted when in need. He faked visas. He faked every other document. He was an enabling fake. He was the minister of travelling. He used to issue visas to people who travelled conveniently to different countries in the world with no problems. So we decided we were going to go through that route for me to enter South African. My passport, I still have that passport, with a fake visa from Eric of Kombone Mission. My friend Anyu said he was not interested in that fake visa. At the time that we were ready with the money to pay for the fake visa, Dr. Eric had travelled to Angola. He used to go to Angola and buy things and come and sell them. That's how he made additional money, since faking documents was not an everyday request.

Our money was not enough for both of us to travel. I told my friend, "Since you're not interested in the visa, go ahead. Maybe when you get to South Africa you can find a way and send me some money if you have some. South Africa is a land of milk and honey, we gather. You might get money quicker than here." The Muslim refugee house where we stayed in Windhoek was in touch with another refugee house here in Cape Town. So my friend left for South Africa with that Cape Town refugee house in mind. There was communication between the two centres. There's a price. You just pay the truck driver. He would hide you in the truck and cross you over to Upington, and drop you there, and you can take the bus to Cape Town or to Johannesburg. He arrived safely in Cape Town. The whole idea was for me to stay back, try raising some money, while my friend did the same once he was in Cape Town. If he had something he would find a way of sending that to me so I could join him in South Africa. So my friend went ahead. From the story he told me later, he went to the truck and they hid him inside the truck and smuggled him into South Africa. It was much easier for him than for me.

I waited for Dr. Eric from Kombone Mission while I tried to raise some money as well, and when Eric came back, I went to him and he put his visa in my passport. No, I think what happened was, before Eric went to Angola he had my passport. He had taken my passport to put the visa in. Then he suddenly went to Angola. I was lucky that he came back. I think that's the main reason why I stayed back, as my friend proceeded to South Africa. My friend could not raise any money to send back to me. He did not know that it was difficult to get money. Our initial dream of South Africa as a land of milk and honey did not immediately materialise for him when he got there. I eventually raised some money, enough to pay Eric for the visa, and to pay for my transportation to South Africa. So when Eric came back, and gave me back the passport, I went to what they call the Truck Port in Windhoek. Since I had a visa, I decided to take a small car, a Nissan Bantam. I was with a Nigerian friend, Sam. We are friends till today.

We met in Namibia, staying in the same place. There were two others with us, Prosper and another guy. The Nissan Bantam driver took four of us and put us at the back of the bakkie and drove us. We managed to cross the border. We left Namibia. All along the visa was fine, we were checked, our passports were stamped and we exited into South Africa. The problem that I had when we got to the South African border was not a problem of the visa being fake. According to the immigration officers the visa was fine, but since ours was a visitor's visa, they wanted us to show proof of a return ticket, or at least to show that we had enough money to stay in the country and return to our destinations, without being a burden to the South African economy. But we never had the money. We never had the ticket, neither me nor my friend Sam.

After I came back from Saudi Arabia my intention was to create contacts with Pamol, a company that produces palm oil and other palm products in the South West Region, and the CDC. The idea was for me to explore possibilities for the exportation of banana, rubber and palm oil to Saudi Arabia. Before I left Cameroon, I struck a deal with CDC to serve as a middleman for the products, and they gave me a sample of some of their products that I could market. I had the agreement with me and I had the samples with me as well. All of these things were inside my briefcase. I started thinking how I could use this agreement and the sample products in my favour.

At the borders they said we could not go into South Africa, and insisted the person who had brought us should take us back to the Namibian border. The driver was supposed to take us back to the Namibian border. There was a very long space of forest between the Namibian exit point where the immigration and the customs were. From there you have to drive a long way for you to get to a check point to enter South Africa. I think all of that territory was within Namibia, or was it No Man's Land? The check point was at the beginning of the forest. The driver drove us and got to maybe midway or so before he stopped the car and told us to come down. It was in the middle of nowhere. It was at night, about 1 o'clock in the morning. He dropped us there, at 1 o'clock, in the forest. He physically forced us out of his car. It was very scary. That was one of the scariest experiences I have ever had – being dropped in the middle of nowhere, in no man's land. We hadn't a clue where we were. I felt frightened. Once in a while you find a car drive past but no car would stop. They probably thought we were armed robbers.

It was only after the driver had dropped us, turned his car and driven off that I discovered that my briefcase was gone. I did not take my briefcase. He went with my briefcase. Everything of mine that was important was inside. What I had on me was just a jean, some takkies, a shirt and a jacket. These too had got really old owing to over-usage. Fortunately enough, my passport was inside my jacket, because I had to use it at a check point at the border and that was it. He went with my bag and my briefcase. Sam had his backpack with him and in it was a small blanket.

It was the kind of small blanket that they found in refugee camps. This was in the middle of winter and winter in Namibia is harsher than here in Cape Town, very harsh. You find your lips cracking without warning. We were hungry, cold, I had nothing, Sam had his small blanket, that blanket was not big enough for two people. So we used to fight over it, but the blanket was clearly humbled by the cold. What we did from there was the only thing we could do. We had to jog to keep ourselves warm. We would jog, and when we were tired of jogging, we would sit on stones and try to catch some sleep. But it was difficult to sleep.

I remember this big stone that we met and it was a bit comfortable. We had to sleep on it, and so we were fighting over that little blanket to cover ourselves. Our nostrils were running. It was the kind of cold weather that makes one's nostrils run nonstop. I was beyond very cold. It took us from 1 o'clock in the morning to 8 or 9am to get to the Namibian border. There we encountered another problem. We were a Cameroonian and a Nigerian, and the Namibian border authorities had already checked us out of their country. Our passports had already been stamped to indicate that we had exited. Coming back to Namibia required being granted permission to enter, afresh. We were at a loss on how to go about explaining ourselves. So I told Sam that this was going to be a bigger problem because we did not have legal residence in Namibia. We didn't have a visa to enter the country, our visa having been terminated from the time they stamped exit on our passports. And we didn't have money either. Nor did we have a ticket to show that we could be allowed into the country. It was tough.

So we decided to dodge the immigration checkpoint when we got there. We could not afford to be seen by them. When we saw the checkpoint from afar, we had to go around and fortunately enough, we found a way to go under the barb wire fence and enter Namibia again, undetected. We smuggled ourselves back into Namibia. As much as we wanted to avoid the checkpoint, it was the only place around with a house, so it was the only place we could go to again. The entire place for miles and miles was a vast land with nothing to see. One could see a car like a dot coming on the road in the far distance. There was no place to go, no place to hide, literally. We had no idea where the next town was and after leaving Windhoek, it was all like a desert. There were no houses, we had to go back to the check point. That was our only option.

When we went back what we did was we hid ourselves behind the house. It was a long house. We hid ourselves at the back and we stayed there waiting. At one point Sam dozed off because we were so tired. But I couldn't sleep because I knew we were going to get caught. So we hid ourselves there, watching the cars as they passed. Then a driver came with a truck, a delivery van actually. I saw the post office sign on the truck. It was a truck that delivered parcels and mail from South Africa to Namibia and vice versa. It was a South African Post Office Delivery van. The driver packed his van, and went out with his documents to go for whatever at the border.

There was another person in the van. He was Coloured,

just like the Coloureds of Namibia. I had to crawl on my stomach to avoid detection as I moved towards him. When he noticed me, he was frightened. He thought I was coming to rob him, and started shouting. I tried to hush him up, to reassure him that I meant no harm. The man calmed down. I explained to him that we just got repatriated from the South African border, and we had to walk all the way back to the Namibian border post. We were so tired, my friend and I. We didn't know where to go. We were illegal here. We needed to go to South Africa. We had family in South Africa, we told him, and asked him if he could help us.

The man was just a "motor boy", so he hadn't the final say. He said I must hide myself there and wait for him to speak to the driver upon his return. So I waited, and told Sam to do the same. We just waited. The driver came and this man spoke to him. They called us, we came and they opened the door. It was a van whose door was by the side. He opened it as if he was checking something, then backing the border post officers he beckoned us and told us to go inside. When we jumped inside, he closed the door. It was dark inside. It was a sealed van. There was no air inside, no light, just dark. But it was warm. That was a good thing.

Inside the van were parcels, big boxes and other things. As Sam went inside and they closed the door, I could not find Sam again. I touched and spoke but Sam would not answer. I started being afraid. Then I discovered that Sam had actually fixed a place for himself. He hid himself because he was afraid that if they opened the van at the borders they would find him. Well, after some time, I shouted again, much louder. Then he shouted back and he told me where he was hiding. He hid himself underneath the boxes. I did the same. So the boxes were on me and between me. We stayed there. We could not sleep even though it was warmer than outside. We could not sleep because we were afraid, and because of the inconvenience too. We did not even know when the guys stopped at the border. Well, we could have known if we wanted to but we were focused on our own problems. So I didn't know when we passed the border. The only thing I heard was the door opening and we hid ourselves further inside. We thought it was the immigration officers, so when we heard the door opening, we hid ourselves further. Then we heard the driver call out, "Hey my friends, we've arrived in Upington. Welcome to South Africa." Wow!! That's how relieved we were. I played back again and again, his words. "We've arrived in Upington. Welcome to South Africa." Those were the most reassuring words I had heard for a long time. It was what I had dreamed of for over a year to hear. I have cherished those words till this date.

Chapter 8

Graced by South Africa

We paid the driver and his assistant a very meagre amount. They were very good to us. When the driver put us in the van back at the Namibian border, he asked us how much money we had. We said not much, I had a few Namibian dollars. I didn't know about Sam, people never tell the truth about their finances. But I gave the driver 100 or so Namibian dollars which was equal to R100. The balance that I had was enough for me to take a bus from Upington to Cape Town. They dropped us off at the bus stop, at the taxi rank and helped us identify a bus. We paid and then we were in the bus for Cape Town. It was almost evening when we got to Upington, so we had to travel during the night to Cape Town. I don't know where the bus dropped us off in Cape Town. Till today, I am still looking for that place. I still want to go back to that place where I was dropped. After staying in Cape Town for close to twenty years, I still don't know where it is that they dropped us that night.

It was about 4 am in the morning when we arrived in Cape Town for the first time that day nearly two decades ago. I didn't know what to do. I had a couple of banknotes in Namibian dollars in my pocket. When the bus dropped us off at that elusive spot, the driver told us we could take a taxi to anywhere from there. Actually, it was us who asked the driver to drop us there so that we could get a taxi because we never wanted anyone in the bus to know that we didn't have documents. We were afraid - anything could happen. So he dropped us there and said we could get a taxi to anywhere in Cape Town. We approached a Coloured man who had a meter taxi, and gave him the address we were given in Namibia to take us to a refuge for stranded travellers, similar to where we were staying in Windhoek. The cabdriver told us to pay R200. It turned out that Sam didn't have money. Sam never had anything on him. I had my Namibian dollars in my pocket as change, and when this cabdriver said R200 I told him I had Namibian dollars, and asked him if that was fine. He said yes. I thought I had 200 but actually, I had 20. So the cabdriver took us and dropped us at the place and I took out the 20 and gave it to him. He was furious and took out a gun. He wanted to shoot me, if I didn't hand over the 200 Namibian dollars. I must pay his money. I started shouting. We started shouting. It was 6 or 7am in the morning. The owner of that night shelter came out and saved us. He calmed the cabdriver down, explained matters to him, and they reached an understanding for the cabdriver to come by on the weekend and collect his money. The owner of the shelter welcomed us. At that time there were very few refugees in South Africa from Africa. I met a couple of people inside, especially from Nigeria, but mostly from Tanzania and Kenya. Anyu, my friend and fellow adventurer from Cameroon, was not there. Later on I discovered that a good family man, one Muslim, came and pitied him, took him in, and gave him a room in his house so he was staying with that man. Our night shelter was in Hanover Park, the area where they fight all the time. Hanover Park is notorious for its gangs.

My friend was staying in Manenberg. He used to come to the shelter to check for me, so we caught up with each other in a couple of days. He was not making money at that time, so he could not help me raise the money to pay the cabdriver. I survived and was able to pay the money I owed the cabdriver through a practice common to the shelter for the stranded. People used to come around there, and take us to clean their cars or go and clean their gardens, or dig trenches or whatever, odd jobs they had. Once in a while we would render such services and they would reward us with R2, R5, R10 and sometimes R20 even.

Once I had paid off my debt, I started saving whatever money came my way, surviving on the barest minimum possible. R20 was a lot of money. It had a lot of value. In those days if you sent R1000 to Cameroon, it fetched you something like 150.000 francs. That was a lot of money in those days, and you could do a lot with it in South Africa or Cameroon. A dollar was like R3.40. That is how strong the Rand was then. With R20 you could live for a whole week. The train in those days was something like R1, or less, just a couple of cents. Now I don't know how much a train ride is, I've not used the train for a long time now. Money had a lot of value at that time.

Most of the others who lived at the shelter with me used to go out in the morning. They would go to Cape Town and sell sweets, chips and other things. The most popular business that they did was selling potato chips in packets. One of the guys from Tanzania told me that if you buy a box of Simba chips with 48 packs for R38, you can sell it for R48, R1 a pack that is, and make R10 profit. I didn't know how I was going to raise R40 to buy and retail. But I continued doing what I was doing to pay my debts and save a little after subsistence. In that refugee camp, there was no hot water in the winter. You had to wash yourself as if you were in a military camp. You had to get up at 4am and take a cold shower and you had to sleep on a mattress that was as slim as a razor blade. The blankets were just as slim. We may have been seeking refuge, but there wasn't much refuge for us from the harshness of life in winter.

When we got there Sam stayed in that place for about two or three days and disappeared. I only met him again in Cape

Town when we started trading. I had nowhere to go. Maybe he knew someone who was already here at that time, so he disappeared. And when I met him, he tried to sweet tongue his way out of his share of what he owed me for having paid the cabdriver myself. When I got my R40 I had to follow this Tanzanian camp mate to Cape Town -I think his name was Ernest- so that he could show me where to go and buy the chips for sale. When in Rome, do what the Romans do. That was the only thing we knew. I followed Ernest early one morning. We walked to the train station in Landsdowne. He had his money for a ticket. I didn't have money for a ticket. I had just enough to go and buy the box of chips. He indicated to me to follow the train route to Cape Town, including where to alight from the train. So he took the train and went, and I started walking from Hanover Park in the same direction of his train. I was following the railway line, dodging trains, because I didn't want to miss the way by following the main road.

That was a long trip. It was a long walk to go to Cape Town, and I arrived after midday. I had to smuggle myself out of the station without a ticket. No one would have believed me if I told them I had walked along the railway line all the way from Hanover Park. I came out of the train tracks at Woodstock in order to enter the main road, where I continued to walk the rest of the distance into the city centre. It was the only way of avoiding paying for a ticket, a Good Samaritan told me. At the city centre, I got to the taxi rank. I searched until I met Ernest. Then he took me to buy the chips and I bought the box of chips. I still remember the flavour that I bought. It was fruity chutney. There were different flavours and there were popular flavours and unpopular flavours. I didn't know, so I bought the unpopular flavour. It took me three days to sell out. There was no profit because I had to eat some of it, but I recovered my capital.

That same day I was too tired to attempt walking back the way I had come, so I had to pay about R1 for the train. The third day I raised my capital, and then I discovered the trick. I came up with this concept to meet all the guys who were struggling like me, and to persuade them to go and buy chips together. If we were four, I think I put together about four of us, we could each buy a different flavour of chips and then share them. It meant that each of us had at least 10 packs of each flavour to trade with, rather than limiting ourselves to the flavour that our R40 or R38 could afford. Each of us could have BBQ, tomato sauce, smoked beef and Mexican chilli flavours, then mix them and in that way could attract a wider pool of customers. I made a profit of R10 from that outing. I was so excited. That was the first income I made in South Africa. At the end of the day I made R10. I could pay for the train. The next day I met my friends again. I had saved R8 that day. On the second day I think I sold two boxes and I made a profit of R20. By the end of that week I was able to go out there and buy four boxes of my own chips, with my own money. I did not have to ask those guys to come with me so we could mix.

The second week I was able to buy cold drinks because chips go well with cold drinks. I bought a 6-pack of coke and cream soda, and I got a bucket so I could buy ice to cool the drinks. I was well equipped to take my chips and cold drinks around, seeking the attention of customers. At the taxi rank I shuttled from one taxi to another selling to whoever cared to buy. I think it was the third week that I thought I should employ someone to help me because my business was getting bigger and bigger, and I was convinced that I could make more money if I recruited an assistant. I wanted to target particular spots in the taxi rank, especially where people queued to take the taxi. I wanted to be able to place about eight to ten boxes of chips and two big boxes of cold drinks at such a strategic location, with an assistant to handle the stand while I continued running around, shuttling between taxis, selling. That way, I got to do more sales and also make more money. I also felt it was much easier for people to identify a particular spot where they knew they could go to get what they wanted and where they could get a wider variety of flavours. It worked! Very well! So I opened another stand, and another one. I then had to make sure I supervised the stands, collected money and bought more stock as flavours ran out. But I did not stop running around selling too. It was easy to get girls to assist me as many girls from the locations or townships always came looking for jobs. Somehow girls from the townships were always looking for jobs. Today, in Cape Town, you find lots of people with stands – coloured whites and blacks alike -, but the idea of stands was first introduced by us foreigners. I discovered that there was a lot of money to be made doing in what I was doing.

I made so much money with this business that I moved out of the shelter. My friend Anyu and I decided to rent a room in someone's house in Sherwood Park, right next to Manenberg, noted for gangsterism. I think we were paying R400 a month for the room. Today, I rent out similar rooms elsewhere for over R2000 per month. My friend was not a business minded person. He just wanted to work. When he was staying with that family, they helped him. He went to do a security course for a few weeks, and began working as a security officer, while I was doing my business.

I decided to go to school to do the same course as my friend. I did the grade E and grade D for two weeks. I wanted to do Grade C but I decided to go and look for a job. At the end of the training, companies came to campaign for workers. When I finished those courses I was the best student in the history of the school. When companies came to look for workers they always wanted to take the top students. I was faced with a problem of choice: which company to work with. I finally chose one company, Federal Guarding in Salt River. At the time my stands were still running at the taxi rank. The girls were there selling on the stands while I was going to school. When I left school I would pass by my stands to ensure everything was okay, collect money and buy new stock. When I started working, I worked only at night. I would go to my security job at night, in the morning I would go home, catch a bit of sleep, and then go to the taxi rank to assist the girls on the stands.

I did that job for three months and I raised enough money to bring my wife from Cameroon to Cape Town. So after five months in South Africa, I brought my wife. It was not just her. I also got a visa for her cousin, so they came together. Both the visas and her flight ticket cost a lot of money, but I could afford it. Her cousin lived with us for a while before moving on. After that I decided to stop working as a security officer. I think I did it for four months. I achieved what I wanted. It was not an ideal job. It's a job for a lazy person. It's a job for people who are satisfied with peanuts. You do certain things because you want to achieve certain goals. I did that to bring my wife and have enough money to improve my business.

From the stand for chips and cold drinks I moved on to selling caps, face caps, sun glasses and related things. I opened another stand for these items, but the chips and cold drinks stand was still there. This was my version of diversification. The business flourished and I decided to open a third stand. It was when I opened the third stand that I stopped the chips and cold drinks. There were too many people doing chips and cold drinks, so the market became saturated, especially as we were targeting the same clientele. The foreigners had introduced the idea of stands, and now everyone, every local, was thinking of nothing else but chips and cold drinks stands. It was like mimicry, and I hate mimicry. I adore originality, and want to keep advancing all the time. So from the face caps I went to bags, ladies handbags, school bags and similar items.

    I had one stand in Cape Town at the back of the post office. Towards December I needed to employ more than five people to help me there. It was not such a big stand, but it was very busy. I was selling three items on that stand: sun glasses, face caps and secret socks, the sort that ladies wear, the light ones. These were three items that attracted customers to the stand round the clock, especially during busy seasons such as Christmas. I needed three ladies to stand on the three items. I needed others to watch that nothing was stolen. I needed someone to collect the money, because it was so busy. Customers had to queue up. We were making more than 100% profit. I would buy a pair of sun glasses for R6 and sell them for R25 or R30. What I bought for R10 I sold for R40. There was so much money in that thing. I would buy a bag of secret socks with 500 of them inside. I used to buy for about R300 and I would sell it for R1200, R1400. Most people did not know it and these were the items I discovered that sold a lot. I restricted myself but others who were not sharp enough were not making money. I was making money. At one time I had four stands on the Grand Parade.

    Seemingly that was the smallest, but it was making the most money because there I specialized. The other stands were bags and things like that. At that time, if you could save say R5000 at the end of the month you were a millionaire. R5000 saved was a lot of money. If you heard that someone was making R5000 that was a lot. If you compare it to when we worked as a security guard, we were getting something like R40 a shift and if you worked nonstop and without much rest, we ended up with R1200 a month. And, that was if you really worked hard. The average worker in South African was earning R700 - R800 a month then. They worked their normal shifts. But we used to go the extra mile to ask for more shifts. Sometimes I used to work over the weekends, because I knew it doubled the amount I took home. When my stands were taken care of, I used to go to work on Friday and only come back on Tuesday. I worked day and night, so I could save R6000 to R7000 a month. Sometimes I saved as much as R10,000, especially during peak periods such as December. In December you could make R1000 profit a day on those stands. There was a lot of money to be made from those stands. But everything has got an end.

We moved to a flat in Kensington. My wife came to South Africa and we had a baby. I was still staying with my friend, Anyu. I am a man - if I see someone who needs help, and I can help, I will do it. I had a problem with my friend. We rented a 2 bed room flat. He had one room and I had the other one. But most of the time, my friend could not understand why I was so generous to others. I was the only Abakwa man in Cape Town at the time. When we came here we met only one other Cameroonian. His name was Jock. He was Bayangi like my friend Anyu. Anyu met him on the train by coincidence. Jock was staying in Khayelitsha, a black township, at the time. He had been in South Africa for about two years before us and he had a South African ID. He came at the time when Mandela was about to be released from prison. I don't know how, but he had his ID already and was staying in Khayelitsha. At the time that Tata Mandela was released from Robben Island, and the ANC was on the verge of taking over government, many black South African activists who were in exile started trooping back home. Many of them had to apply for IDs in preparation for elections. The African immigrants, like Jock who came in at the time, only had to adopt South African parents' names to apply for South African IDs. I think that's how he got his ID, and that explains why he was living in Khayelitsha. That is how many immigrants became citizens at that time. It was when Anyu was coming back from work that they met by chance. When you see your own brother you know, you just know. So they met each other. We took Jock out of Khayelitsha. He was kind of lazy then, not very ambitious. He came over, he stayed with us for some time, we helped him, and he went to security school and started working.

Anyu was a student all the time, forever wanting to study. He's forever a student, even now. So he started going to school! Technikon, university, whatever. He tried to encourage Jock to go to school as well, but Jock would not go. He was more interested in making a little money, drinking with women, and enjoying life with little means. He was completely without ambition. He lived his life for the moment. He was also very over bearing. You would help him but he wouldn't recognize it. He just thought we were stupid. That's what Jock was. He stayed with us for quite a while. He never paid for anything, nor did he buy food. Instead, we gave him money and helped him with his training as a security guard. We started having problems with him, because he wanted to take control instead of fitting into the lives and patterns of those who were helping him. At the end of the day we sent him away. But under Anyu's guidance, he went to school, obtained a degree or two and today is a responsible family man, gainfully employed.

We had actually started building a small Cameroonian community with the coming of a few other Cameroonians. We were very few, but at least we could meet and chat about home once in a while, and share tit bits from back home. This eventually led to the formation of a Cameroon gathering in Maitland where we met once a month to share information from home while boozing the "Camer" way, as we are fond of referring to in Cameroon. This eventually grew into the Cameroon Association of today in Cape Town. But there was still something missing in my life: I had almost forgotten how to speak my home language, Pinyin, as for a very long time, since the day I left Victoria or Tiko, I had not had the privilege of sustaining a conversation for more than a few minutes with anyone in my dialect. At that time, I decided to bring my kid brother, Moma, who had just passed his GCE O Levels then, to join me in Cape Town. He was the one who helped me regain the Pinyin dialect that I had lost thus far. Moma was very young at the time. But he was and still is very humble, respectful, caring, hardworking and enterprising. He fitted in perfectly and has never given me any reason to doubt his commitment to these virtues. His humility, dedication and hard work paid off: today he is an electrical engineer with two Masters degrees working with an International oil company. He has a good job that takes him to many countries around the world. He is now married, owns a couple of properties in Cape Town and in Cameroon. But with his success, he has never lost his virtues, he is still very humble, respectful and helps me a lot to look after the family. He is the one brother, son and friend that I trust wholly. We are really close. We do a lot of things together. It is Moma's qualities that encouraged me to bring our other brothers, cousins and in-laws to South Africa too.

Doma follows Moma directly in biological terms. He too has made me very proud. The day I picked him up at Cape Town International Airport, we went directly to the University of the Western Cape to register him for a degree programme in Biomedical Science. He was late for school as his visa took longer than expected. Three years on he graduated with a BSc in Biomedical Science. One night he came home to show me an admission letter for a Masters degree programme in Public

Health in Lund University in Sweden. That was even before his final results in UWC. With Moma's assistance, we did all we could to get him to Lund. After his MSc degree he decided to return to Cameroon to get married and do evangelical work for a year before going in for his PhD. He has achieved all that and is now busy looking for a school to do his PhD. What is striking about Doma is his faith in God. He started All Pinyin For Jesus while in Sweden and is using it to spread God's word and bring many to Christ with the use of social media. When he came to Cape Town, I gave him R500 as pocket money. But with that money, instead of spending it, he invested it. He decided to go with other Cameroonians to buy and sell products on the streets on weekends and during holidays. Most Cameroonians in Cape Town do something called pitching, a form of hawking where they buy from wholesale shops and go round town selling to people on the streets. I am credited with being the founder of this form of business as I started it in Cape Town. So instead of me paying Doma's fees and giving him pocket money, he would come and give me a lot of money especially at the end of the holidays, for me to add and pay his fees. He would even buy food for the house, buy things for the kids and even send stuff and money to family any time I visited Cameroon. Even when he went to Sweden, we only paid for his accommodation and pocket money for the first three months or so. Doma is so hard working, independent and caring. The first decent laptop I ever owned, the one I'm typing on right now, was a gift from Doma while he was in Sweden. Moma and Doma, how I wish everyone in the family could learn from you, from your shining example. But as they say, not everyone is the same, not even twins can be the same.

Nkang and Nyam are not like Moma and Doma. When I brought these two to Cape Town, it was because our father insisted I take them away from him, so that he may live longer.

They had become thorns in his flesh, causing him sleepless nights with their senseless demands, wayward lifestyle, lack of seriousness in school, and in anything they did and even threats on Dad's life when he didn't condescend to their bidding. I thought a new environment would do them some good. But as they say you can never wash off the leopard's spots. Nkang is the same today after living in Cape Town for over ten years. He came to South Africa at about the same time with Taanji. I enrolled them in Pinelands College on the same day and paid their fees for the term. Nkang abandoned school, left my house, he wanted independence. Today Taanji is working and doing his Masters programme in electrical engineering. I have spent a lot of money on Nkang, including opening up a fashion shop in a shopping mall worth over R130,000 for him, but all those efforts have gone in vain. He is on his own, still pitching on the streets to take care of his bills. Nyam is better off today after leaving Nkang's company. He refused to go to school, he wanted to do business. But with his brother Nkang beside him in Cape Town, nothing happened. But since he moved to Johannesburg, and started a small shop selling computer accessories, he has since changed. He is making money now in his shop and car sales business. He told me last week that he is ready to buy a house in Abakwa, if I can help him to find one. What bothers me about these two is that they are still single at over 30 years of age. Marriage somehow makes a man more responsible. I have a few other irresponsible brothers and sisters in Cameroon who behave just like Nkang. But as our late father used to say, "when the time to stool comes, you will look for the toilet". I hope the younger ones learn from Moma and Doma.

So with Moma, other Pinyinians started coming into South Africa. I had paved the way, I was the torch bearer. All those who came in those days, they came because I paved the way. I had to help in one way or the other to facilitate their coming. News travels very fast. I remember the first time I went home, the time I went incognito, under a different name and passport, for my mother's funeral, I became an unofficial consultant. Young people and parents who wanted their kids to travel to South Africa came knocking, asking for information, assistance, etc. So the Pinyin community in Cape Town and in Johannesburg grew at an alarming rate; I remember I used to receive them frequently, sometimes three at a time, in Cape Town as well as when I was in Johannesburg. The early comers were more disciplined, hardworking, responsible and respectful. People like Esa, Igni, Rob, Ernie, Johnny, small wonder they are all Doctors, PhDs, today; Allo, Jogy, Julio, Wally, Mickey, Eddy, Cy, etc. All these early comers are very successful today. They joined me to start the small Pinyin community that today has grown tremendously. Pinyin is a small village, but it now has one of the biggest and strongest cultural groups in Cape Town and Johannesburg. PIFAM (Pinyin Family Meeting) is highly respected as a group - a progressive and development-conscious family meeting group - in South Africa and beyond. Today there are over 350 registered members of PIFAM in Cape Town and Johannesburg. There are many others who are not registered or who have been dismissed from the Association because of arrogance, dishonesty or non-commitment. With numbers come problems, tensions and indiscipline. The newcomers are not like the early comers, maybe it is youthful exuberance; a good number of them are lazy, disrespectful, irresponsible, and lack ambition and focus. Some want to take short cuts, but what you think are short cuts in life, always become the longest roads to travel.

    Given my willingness to help Cameroonians in Cape Town, they started directing every new comer to my stand, to meet me for help. Even Cameroonians with the means were good at bringing every stranded Cameroonian in Cape Town to my stand. Sometimes I went away to buy as I used to do every now and again, and upon returning, I would find someone sitting, waiting for me to help out. There were several other Cameroonians who had stands just like me, but few of them were inundated with demands to help the way I was. So my house, our house, became like a refugee camp again. I always took those stranded Cameroonians home and Anyu would look at me in total disbelief. He could not understand why I did things like that. I had so many Cameroonians that I helped, some of them have since moved on to the USA, Australia and other countries. The bad thing with helping these Cameroonians is that they didn't seem to appreciate it. Certainly, this was true of the few that I can remember- so many came to live with me. I paid for training. Many of them then went out to work, and earned money enough to enable them to go out and look for their own places. For others, those who wanted to work as restaurant attendants or whatever, I paid for their hospitality training. For some of them, I even gave them money to pay as deposit for their own accommodation. Then, others, who wanted to do business, I gave them capital. That's what I used to do, and the money was there at the time for me to do things like that.

My friend could not understand why, at any given time, there were more than two people staying in our place, sleeping in the lounge. It was because of me. I took them in. My friend got tired and decided to move out. He left me in the flat, and went and looked for his own place.

We have remained friends, notwithstanding his moving out. We are still together, it's just that here you cannot actually keep the kind of closeness that we would have wanted because of each other's commitments. But we are still very much together. I go to visit him and he comes to visit me, and there are occasions, like when my mum or my dad passed away, when he was there to support me. When he lost his mum, I was there to support him. Here, we are like family. That is what we call each other. He has got his own shortcomings, but I treat people the way I see them. I don't analyse friends. Anyu is not very tolerant. But I get along with him. Anyu has actually added more value to my life. We complemented each other, especially on the journey from Cameroon to here. Morally, materially and otherwise we complemented each other. If it wasn't for him I wouldn't be here and if it wasn't for me, I am not sure he would be here either. When I go to Cameroon, sometimes I pay his folks a visit. When Anyu left, it was as if he opened the door for more people. I remember these two Abakwa boys, childhood friends from Mankon who decided to travel to SA, Mamo and Ndeh. I went to meet them on my stand one day. Abandoned there by one Pakossi, was a Cameroonian from Douala married to a Bakossi lady. This couple met us in Namibia. They had the means. Pakossi could have given Mamo and Ndeh shelter, but he chose to bring them to my stand instead. I welcomed them, took them home and they slept in the lounge. I paid for their training as security guards and they started working. They were now making some money. So I said they could move into the room Anyu had vacated and contribute to the rent, now that they were earning some money. They moved in quite alright, but when it was time to pay the rent, they complained that they didn't have any money to contribute. I knew they were making enough money to contribute to paying the rent. They stayed with me for over a year, and didn't even buy food. I expected them to contribute, but when they repeatedly didn't I gave up trying. I didn't bother.

Ndeh and Mamo were staying with me when my son was

born. Finally, although reluctantly, they left my house when I decided to bring my brother and my wife's brother from Cameroon. They moved out of the room, left and got their own place.

Mamo, one of the guys, had family in the United States. The sister was there, and the mother too. He also had a sister in Cameroon who was married to another Cameroonian, a school mate of hers, with aspirations of using his marriage to her as his gateway to the US. Mamo travelled to the States, eventually, after his sister and husband in Cameroon joined him in Cape Town. I was the one who assisted him with his visa to the US. We had become like family, despite their distasteful attitude to their obligations to pay rent and contribute to our collective subsistence. I was already doing the business that I am doing today, with an office in Wynberg. That's how much I had grown. I had an office in Wynberg. One day Mamo came to me and said he needed some money, R20,000 for him to get a bank statement to enable him get a visa. He was applying for a student visa.

I was surprised when Mamo approached me for help. He was the one who left my house and never ever came back. His friend Ndeh used to come once in a while and bring things to the kids, but Mamo never ever came. He didn't even call. Yet, when his interest was at stake he came to me for help and I gave him the R20,000. I was making money at the time, good money. I gave him R20,000 to put in his account to facilitate his visa process. I was afraid he might take the money and go away with it for good. But even he surprised me. He got the visa, and returned my money before he left. But Mamo shall always be Mamo. Ever since he got his visa and left South Africa, I have not heard from him. Sometimes when people leave they create new friends and they forget about the old ones. He left his sister and husband behind. She was diagnosed with a terminal disease, and became intermittently sick. She was so sick that her boyfriend considered her a problem, a headache, and abandoned her. She knew no one else in Cape Town but us, so my wife and I would go and take care of her. She was staying in a tiny little room in Salt River. She became virtually our responsibility. Her name was Diane, and her illness only got worse until finally she passed away. She didn't die in Cape Town. She died at home in Cameroon. After the doctor in Cape Town announced that she had less than a month to live, I arranged for her to be repatriated. We got to hospital, signed the necessary documents, accompanied her to Johannesburg, put her on a flight home and communicated to her family that they needed to collect her from the airport. Jane did not last long when she got home. She died within a week of going home. But she died with dignity and amid family and friends at home. She didn't receive the love she had expected from Mamo and the rest of her family in the US. Even Peter, her husband, had abandoned her. They behaved as if she didn't exist.

Those are some of the things you do with people. When you leave home, when you go out of your village, region or country, you create family, and that family is not like blood relations, but it is family all the same. I was that kind of a person. I always like to help others. Many Cameroonians have passed through here, benefited from my assistance and gone off to various parts of the world. There are so many of them in Hong Kong, Singapore, Japan, China, Australia and even Cameroon and other African countries not to mention the US and Europe. I went to Cameroon a while back and met someone who is now big in business. We called him General. I got him a visa to travel to South Africa. He came to Cape Town at the same time as my wife's brother. They were friends and came together. Both of them stayed with us for a long time. In those days there were no cell phones. Indeed, the cell phone was still only being introduced in South Africa at the time. It was still not common. It was General who told me that there was something called the cell phone. He said Pa Yong wanted one. Pa Yong was a very renowned businessman in Abakwa, one of the foremost businessmen in the region. He owns many businesses including schools, soccer academy, soccer team and even a university. General asked if I could get a cell phone for us to send to Pa Yong, who was married to his sister. I investigated into shops from which I thought I could buy such stock for sale from. I finally discovered someone at Sea Point who was selling the banana Nokia phones, so nicknamed because they were long and curved just like a banana. So I bought the two he had left in stock. They were well packaged in cute boxes.

I can't remember how much I bought them for. We sent the phones to Pa Yong and Pa Yong refunded the money to my uncle in Cameroon, just as I had indicated he should. I was so surprised that he was requesting those phones for Cameroon, as to the best of my knowledge, there was no network in Cameroon for making and receiving cell phone calls. Till today, I don't know what he did with the phones. That was the first deal I made between South Africa and Cameroon, and I discovered that I could make lots of money trading between South Africa and Cameroon. I made more than 200% profit with those phones.

I've lived through two eras – the era of no cell phones, I lived it and did business during that time – and now we are in a more sophisticated era where you have more gadgets of communication which just make things easier. If I think of those days back home when business and communication were more through letters and word of mouth, things were much slower. A business partner had to wait for a letter to arrive by post, or worse still, for you to come to them on foot. And I remember how often I used to have to go to the post office to make a phone call to someone in France. That was a big thing and you had to save a lot of money for that. And if someone heard that you were talking on the phone in those days – we are talking about the 90s or pre-nineties –, if someone heard you were talking on the phone, it was something strange, something special, a luxury few could afford, even among the elite. It was like you were a white man, because it was only in the movies that such things happened. And how we survived at that time, I can't begin to imagine, but we did.

When I was trading with Nigeria, maybe they had phones in those shops that we used to buy from, but it just didn't occur to me that I could even take the number to call from Cameroon, because I knew that it was not going to work or if it worked, that the costs would be too exorbitant to contemplate. So even if I bought goods from Nigeria and they were faulty, I would have to physically travel back to Nigeria to have them replaced. Sometimes you go back and you find that, it would have been easier for me to phone and find out if they had the stuff or not. It would have made life much easier, but you had to go all the way back from Cameroon to Nigeria to find out that this customer doesn't have this thing. I have already mentioned when I went to Nigeria for the first time. It was to go and buy my robe. I assumed that you normally found that robe in Onitsha or even in Aba, even though I'd never been there before. So if I knew that there was no robe in Onitsha, I wouldn't have gone with the kind of money that I went with, but for me to know at that time that there were no robes in Onitsha, I had to go myself. But these days you know what you can do, you can go to the internet, you can go to websites, check the address on the internet and what they advertise and there are so many ways that you can find out. So life is much easier these days. When we got lost at sea for a couple of days, no one ever knew what was happening to me. When I used to leave Cameroon and go to Nigeria there was no communication between me and anybody. The only thing that would make people worry about you is if on the day you were supposed to come back, you didn't – that is, if they had prior knowledge of when you were to be back. They'll start asking, where is this guy? In those days someone could go and die and stay for months before they knew that the person had died. There was no means of instant communication of the type we wallow in today.

When I left for South Africa, I spent sixteen months travelling and it was also sixteen months of non-communication with any relatives. At the time I knew it was probably more to do with not wanting to communicate, because in the chambers where I used to practice law in Abakwa there was a phone. I could have phoned the landline and left a message for my parents, my wife or whoever. But I was held back by the thought of having achieved nothing to report back. Even in Zaire I knew that if I went to the embassy and asked them, they could let me phone. If I had a cell phone at that time I would have been tempted and even communicated with my wife. I should have phoned her and a couple of people. And when I arrived here in South Africa, it was different in the sense that the cell phone was just being introduced into South Africa. It wasn't the way it is now.

As already indicated, I was not using the cell phone at the time I bought the phones for Pa Yong. Maybe because I didn't have a use for it at that time or it was too expensive for me to use and things like that. But, what I can remember now is that when I started doing business, it wasn't possible for me to be sitting here talking to someone else and giving directives to my workers in the office. It never used to happen in those days.

Even here in South Africa when I started doing business, I was running an office and, well, even though a manager might have a cell phone, not everyone had a cell phone. It was still difficult to liaise with your workers when you were not there. It was difficult at that time to communicate and most of the time the means of communication would be to drive all the way - if I wanted to know what was happening in my office for instance. I could phone the landline in South Africa, which was far much better equipped in this regard than Cameroon. At the time that I started business, every office had a phone, you could call the landline using a public phone, but individual communication with someone who is out of the office was not possible.

The first cell phone I bought for myself was when I was promoted as a manager. It was a big thing. Cell phones were expensive then. I remember I bought an Alcatel one touch easy. It was a big phone with a long antenna and the phone, at that time, was R1000 or more. It was supposed to be the cheapest phone on the market. At the time I bought it, it was like only managers could buy phones. It's not like today. Well, at the time, very few people had phones. So even if you had a phone you could not be as busy as we are now, because few would call your cell phone, since not many people had a cell phone in those days. The phone at that time was more a class thing, not so much a necessity. Today, having a cell phone is not a class thing anymore. It's not a luxury. It's a necessity. It is something you're compelled to have. In my business, if an employee came to me and did not have a cell phone or a contact number I would not hire them. This is because in this job we deal with money and if you take money or merchandise and you run away, there will be no way for me to contact you. So if someone comes looking for a job, he must be able to give us contactable references. That is how important cell phones are today. And it makes life much easier. I used to have so many offices in Johannesburg and Durban. I could stay here in Cape Town and run a meeting in Durban. I used to do that. I would call all the managers, put them on the speaker phone and we communicated. Sometimes we did conference calls. I used to do conference calls with my managers in various cities. So communication has become so easy these days with the advent of all these facilities and it just makes life much easier. The introduction of smart phones is taking things to yet another level of ease. We are living in exciting times in terms of technological innovations; what in yesteryears would have passed for witchcraft is today understood or explained away in the name of technology.

The positive side of the cell phone is that it makes life much easier. You can be anywhere and you use the cell phone to do just about anything. I use the cell phone to phone and speak to my sisters, I speak to my brothers and I speak to relatives at home. When I got to South Africa, the only way that I knew that my mother was dead was when I received a letter from Cameroon. I received that letter when she was dead for more than a year. But that kind of thing is not going to happen today because of the cell phone, that's the positive side of cell phones. When my father was sick, every step of the way, I was following up and as soon as he died, it didn't take even five minutes for me to know that he had died. In fact, I learnt of his death much earlier and faster than his neighbours in the village did. So, at the end of the day, the cell phone is a big positive, relation-wise, especially for those of us outside. It helps us keep in touch with the family and with friends back home. Business-wise, it makes things much easier, because if I have to drive all the way from Goodwood where I live presently to Bellville where I own a property which I have given out on rent, like when I have an emergency, all I need to do is call someone that I know who can sort it out on his cell phone and tell him to go to such a place and sort this out, he will go and do it. And these are short distances within the same city. It is even more fulfilling sitting here in South Africa and running my businesses in Cameroon, especially if founded on relationships of trust, or running my businesses in South Africa, while in Cameroon, just by using the phone.

If I had had a cell phone at the time I was in Saudi Arabia I would have called Cameroon to investigate the companies that exported fruits and cash crops from Africa. The whole idea, back then, was for me to go back to Cameroon and be an agent between Cameroon and Central Africa, buying and exporting to Saudi Arabia. It was that one idea that made me head back to Cameroon, but when I got back, things were not the way I thought they were. Had I known, if it was like today, I wouldn't have done that. I would have called Cameroon and called people to investigate them and check how easy it was to get an import and export license. But, I couldn't do that. It would have been better if there was a cell phone, because it has actually made life easier.

Cell phones are not all positive, alas. There are negatives, a lot of them – positive negatives and negative negatives. Lying is not always negative, contrary to what we tend to think when we hear or uncover a lie. I miss the protection we enjoyed when we lied in the days cell phones were not so handy. With the cell phones these days, it is so difficult for someone to lie, because in those days, you could tell someone I'm going to Johannesburg and that person will never know where you are. That person will assume that you have gone to Johannesburg. But these days what is going to happen if you say you are going to Johannesburg, and you have a cell phone, the person you are going to visit also has a cell phone and I can phone the person and ask 'has this guy arrived'? I can check on you at any time. This is quite unlike in those days when you could lie and do as you like without others finding out.

I have said that cell phones make it difficult for people to lie. That is only at one level, however. On the other hand, it is also possible for people to use cell phones to lie a lot and with negative outcomes both for public and interpersonal relationships. Someone gets up in the morning and intentionally decides to come late to the office. Sometimes the same member of staff sends you the same message almost every morning for a week or more. He says, 'good morning, my train is running late and it's stuck as well, I will be a bit late'. And when I check, this guy has been sending me this message almost every second day for the past two weeks. How can the train be stuck so repeatedly? He is using his cell phone to give an excuse, and when he comes late and I want to punish him he will say but I told you. In previous years, you simply arrived late and you received the sanction. Now, this guy has got an excuse because he has a cell phone and I see this every single day in my business. In those days these things never happened. I think that this is also a negative side of a cell phone.

It is not always a positive thing for people to contact me. It is positive when a call is work related and brings in money. But sometimes you don't even want to answer your cell phone. When I receive a call from home and from a number I don't know, I don't want to answer it because most of the time it is from this far relation who wants to bother you and ask for this and that and in that way, it is a negative. I would imagine that someone who is abroad would be overwhelmed by all of these people who call and ask for me to pick up people at the airport, go and receive them and make space for them to stay with you and study in Cape Town. That is clearly negative. It is not all the time that people will use the cell phone in this way. But I would say that the advantages of the cell phone are more than its disadvantages.

When you leave your home, and you get out of Cameroon, there are people back home that are doing well, even better than you but the fact that you are out of the country is a big thing, and some want to take advantage of you all the time. So the cell phone just makes it easier for them to take advantage of you. Imagine one of my uncles putting 200 francs in his phone to call me. He is someone that I never used to talk to, someone who refused to pay my school fees of 300 francs. He puts 200 francs in his phone to call me and tell me he just called to greet me, please can you call me back, there's something I want to discuss with you. Or at times they keep beeping and when they beep and you don't call back, that's when they put 200 francs or 100 francs to give you that message. And now you have to call back and when you call back, what do they tell you? It's all about money. They are interested in bleeding you dry.

Back to General whose request for me to purchase cell phones for Pa Yong set me off on this rather long reflection on the impact of cell phones. General went to Hong Kong. Recently I met him in Abakwa. He now owns a very big shop in Ntarinkon. He is very ambitious. I could see it coming. He wanted to save money at all cost when he lived with me in Cape Town. He and a friend of his went into business as a partnership. They bought a Combi and used to go to flea markets everywhere. They were doing the same stand business that I used to do. They rented their own place in Khayelitsha and that's where they made their own money. Paradoxically, it was because of Khayelitsha that they had to leave South Africa. They were robbed so many times and their goods taken that they decided to leave the place and leave South Africa. They took their money and left – first to other countries and then subsequently back to Cameroon. They were only a couple of the many Cameroonians that I helped.

We were forced to move when my landlord gave us notice to leave the flat, complaining that we were accommodating too many people. We moved to Mowbray and occupied one big room. It was like a move down for us, from a two bedroom flat to a room, not because we could not afford a flat, but because we couldn't find one to rent at the time. South Africa was changing. To have a place at that time as a foreigner was not easy. We were lucky to have the flat that I had just lost. It was the intervention of one South African Muslim friend that had helped me acquire that flat. Today things have become easier again for foreigners, but in those days having money was not reason enough to qualify to rent a flat, especially for black foreigners from Africa like myself.

Chapter 9

My Wife Never Understood the Business

I always dreamt of corporate life. Even before my wife came, when I was still staying in Kensington, I worked with a marketing company. That's actually how I got to what I am doing now. There was a guy who used to sell products. His name was Kuze. He sounded very articulate, very professional. One day he asked me why someone with my accomplishments, someone who sounded so persuasive and well educated should settle for selling stuff, doing hawking at bus stations and along the streets. It was then that he revealed to me that he was working for a company. It was a company where he had the prospects to become a manager and run his own business. He started telling me more about the company, and I bought the opportunity. He personally invited me to the office. I went and had an interview, and started working with the company. It was in Maitland, Kensington actually. It was a sales and marketing company. It offered training, and enabled newcomers to go through some stages of training to become a manager in their own office.

When I joined the company, the manager was a white Portuguese South African called Joachim De Paolo. I was there for about three months. Then I did all the standards. It was rare for someone to come and in three months do all of those standards. But I did them because I was ambitious. I wanted to run my own office. I was a trainer at Joachim De Paolo's office for three months, and during that period I built a team of 35 people. Despite that impressive record, or perhaps because of it, Joachim De Paolo didn't want to promote me although I had achieved all the standards. In fact, he refused to promote both me and my trainer, Kuze. He didn't treat us well. So we both left. When we left there was another office somewhere in Observatory that we wanted to go to. The opportunity was there to make money, but Joachim De Paolo wanted us to stay in his office and make money for him. Joachim De Paolo didn't want us to work with another DS Max (Direct Sales Maximizers) franchise. The mother company is Canadian but Joachim De Paolo was sufficiently powerful in South Africa to block us from making any headway by moving into another franchise. At that point I decided to go back to my street trading. I used the opportunity to open many more stands in Cape Town. My trainer left. He was known to come from Durban in South Africa, but he was actually Zimbabwean. Kuze didn't want anyone to know that he was from Zimbabwe, not even me. We had become very good friends. He went to Johannesburg where he tried and failed to get to other offices of the company. Joachim De Paolo kept blocking every move we made.

The corporate world has got some fowl play that you would not imagine! For no good reason, this guy blocked us with impunity. There is no law that says I cannot start my own business or use my skills with another office manager. I did not steal from him. We didn't commit any crime. We left because we achieved the required standards and he didn't promote us. But here he was blocking our progress. He did not want us to work with another company and all those offices that we went to were owned by different people under DS Max as franchises. He successfully blocked my trainer in Johannesburg for almost a year. Finally, Kuze decided to come back to Cape Town and go back and work for Joachim De Paolo. He discovered nothing he could do and he wanted an opportunity to work so badly. He informed me once he was back in Cape Town to explain his move. Although I still liked the opportunity, I was determined not to go back to that office. I asked him to let me know if he got promoted. His plan was to open his own office in Johannesburg if and when he was promoted.

About six months down the line, Kuze finally got the promotion he sought. I'm sure Joachim De Paolo finally realized that he would lose him for good if he kept refusing to promote him. In the business, when you promote someone you also make money from his office. So the reason why Joachim De Paolo blocked us from gaining employment with other offices was because he wanted us to come back to his office, so he could benefit from our eventual promotion now that he knew he cannot stop us from becoming managers. Ordinarily he would prefer us to remain trainers in his office so as to build the office for him to make more money. Following his promotion, my trainer returned to Johannesburg where he set up his own office and became his own manager. He also kept in touch with me.

Once Kuze had set up his office in Johannesburg, he invited me to come and work with him. I spoke to my wife about the business. I told her I was going to go to Johannesburg to train and when I get promoted as a manager I will come back to Cape Town and open my own office. It was a difficult decision. It was difficult convincing her. She never wanted that.

My wife never wanted to hear that. Maybe because of insecurity, she never wanted me to leave her with the family in Cape Town. She was pregnant with our third child. I had made up my mind, Johannesburg was not an opportunity to miss. Certainly not after the struggle we had had with Joachim De Paolo. Round about the same time, I brought another cousin, Taning, from Cameroon. Today Taning is in Pretoria, but he was living with us in Cape Town at the time. That's one person

I brought that gave me a lot of problems. Taning was lazy, which came as a big surprise to me, as in Cameroon it was his hard work that stood in his favour when the decision was made for me to bring another relative to Cape Town. Back in Cameroon he used to work hard. He had GCE A levels and was teaching in a primary school. He was making something like 20,000 francs a month and from the 20,000 francs he had a garden. After working for two years he had managed to buy himself two cows. He was also sponsoring his kid sister in the teachers training college. So I could see that given the opportunities he would do his best to exploit them and help the family further. I saved money and brought him here, knowing that he would settle down in record time and start making a life for himself.

I sent Taning to a security school like most I helped. He did not even want to work. He was always sleeping at home. When I brought him from Cameroon, it wasn't because I wanted a babysitter. I wanted someone who could work hard and support the family back home. Now that I had ended up with a babysitter, I wasn't too worried about going to Johannesburg and leaving my wife and children in Cape Town, because I knew my wife would have him to babysit and assist with other things at home. There was also another cousin, who is now in Ghana, staying at home with us. So as far as I could see, there were enough helping hands at home. I knew the family was in good hands. So I decided to leave, and since my wife didn't want to hear of it, I waited until she left for work. I had handed over my stands to Taning and my other cousin to control. She went to work. She was working as a security officer at the time. When she left for work, I left for Johannesburg.

I was in Johannesburg for five months. I was promoted to be manager within that time. It was a fast promotion because it came after four months and three weeks. It was a record in South Africa. I worked with my promoting manager, Kuze, in his Benoni office for two months after my promotion and saved enough money to come back to Cape Town and open my own office in Wynberg. That was a lot of money to open an office at that time. I remember I spent something like R40,000 and I still had to borrow money from my manager. I had to buy furniture and I had to buy this and that. Through my company I had a flat as well, that's the flat I moved my family to, that flat in Wynberg. We were staying there. There's a lot of money in management. You could easily make R1,000 a day.

While I was in the business in Johannesburg I trained a couple of Cameroonians. Taning, the lazy one, I took him up to Johannesburg and trained him. I thought he was going to stay, he didn't. He was too lazy. It was a good thing I took him to Johannesburg, because he never came back to Cape Town. He's now in Pretoria where he's got a computer shop. He's now married, he's got two kids. He brought his wife from Cameroon, he's now taking care of the family. And his wife is studying in the university. He came right after a long time. Today he assists me in helping the extended family back home. He is actually the assistant *chopchair* – successor that is – to my grandfather who died. So he's fine now. When my father died I also went home with him, so you can see that he came right after all.

I trained many more Cameroonians, mostly from my home village of Pinyin. Cameroonians are not patient by nature. They are not patient. They want to have everything today. But in my business, you need to be patient. Sometimes things are really rough but with patience and hard work you'll always make it. Because of their lack of patience, most of those I trained are not in the business today. It is only me and a couple of others who are doing the business. Between the three of us still in the business, we trained more than 40 Cameroonians who have all fallen by the wayside, more or less. Some have gone back to school and some have gone into other businesses, still, some have decided to idle around, become parasites, or chosen the easy way out – become crooks and cheats. Instead of blaming their impatience, when they see you making money, they say you are lucky. It is not luck. It is patience and hard work. They don't want to work and they have no patience.

Patience and hard work, that's all, that's what makes it. There's no luck. There are some people who believe in destiny. I don't think there's any destiny, because you create your own destiny. You've got a choice in life, to choose your own path and that's why I don't have pity for people who choose paths of destruction, because you choose. God gave all of us a reasoning faculty, gave us equal opportunities but some people choose the path of destruction. They choose to be lazy. They choose to be crooks and things like that. There's nothing like predestination. I don't believe in that. Some of those that I trained chose to go back to school, and today some of them have graduated with PhDs. These have become very successful in their different fields. That was their choice. Others chose differently, and have not quite succeeded. I chose to stay on with the business, and have what I have to show for it. We are products of the choices we make in life. Many who believe that only through education is success possible have been going to school after school since they came to South Africa, but with very little to show for it, beyond the accumulation of qualifications. They like books too much. They study and study and keep going for another degree every time. It almost seems as if they are afraid to dare to work. What is the purpose of education if it does not encourage the spirit to dare? Would it be fair for such people to blame their educated inabilities on destiny? Is it fair for them to attribute the success of others to luck?

It was when I was still in that office in Kensington – long before my wife or any other family member joined me in South Africa –, that I received a letter from Cameroon saying that my mother had passed away. My mother had died while I was still in Zaire, but because no one knew where I was, they couldn't inform me. When eventually my uncle found out that I was in South Africa, he sent me a letter informing me of the sad passing of my mother. It was news delayed, but my devastation was total.

When I left Cameroon, no one knew where I was. I only told my wife where I was going to and I told her to swear never to tell anyone and I told my friend who is in the US now, the friend who helped me to leave. Those were the people who knew where I was heading. My father did not know, no one knew, even though I went to tell them bye-bye. I went to greet them. They didn't know I was coming to say bye-bye. I did not tell them but I told people that I was going to the north of Cameroon. I told them I was going to Garoua for business.

My wife went through tough times trying to hide it because at one point she herself gave up. She was afraid that I had died. People thought I had died somewhere. My former boss, Barrister Fet had a phone in his office. So my family thought if someone should know my whereabouts it should be him. They were always bothering him. When I called him to say I am in South Africa, I could hear the relief in his voice. It was as if he was receiving a telephone call from a ghost! My family and friends all used to bug him to tell them of my whereabouts, and when no answers were forthcoming some of them even insinuated that he probably had sacrificed me to *nyongo*, a form of witchcraft that brings in riches if one sacrifices people close to them. I am still closed to Barrister Fet till date. He was like a father to me, a very intelligent, principled, yet caring and friendly man. I learnt a lot about life from him. I sent for my father to come and we talked on the phone but no one told me about my mother's death. When I asked about my mother my father said she was doing fine. They probably didn't want to shock me with news of my mother's death, given the distance that separated Cameroon and South Africa, and how long I had stayed incommunicado. They thought I might take my own life on hearing the sad news of her passing. I was very fond of my dear mother.

I realized that I had to plan to go to Cameroon to do my mother's *crydie*. I came down to Cape Town and opened my Wynberg office in September. In October and November, I had to build the office and pay back my debts to my manager. There was so much money in that business that in the five weeks leading up to Christmas, I made enough money to pay back my debts and still was able to save more than R50, 000. That was the money I took to Cameroon. I had to go and do my own funeral. I went to Cameroon and I went incognito. I never had the required documents to travel out of the country. My friend, Anyu, the one I travelled with to South Africa, came to my aid. I helped him a lot when we left Cameroon and he had nothing. I virtually pulled him to South Africa. He came to my help this time. When we got here, he got married to a Xhosa lady and then applied for permanent residence. So he had permanent residence stamped in his passport. I took his passport to some of these "docky doctors" in Johannesburg, who took out his photo and put mine there as replacement. It was called transplanting. At the time, passports were not computerized, so it was easy doing transplanting. That is how many African immigrants travelled from South Africa to other countries in the world at the time. The few "docky doctors" available at the time were Nigerians. Today this business has developed to employ even Cameroonians who can manufacture a variety of documents including school certificates, birth certificates, drivers' licences and many others. Our friend Dr Eric from Kombone Mission came in handy, when he eventually moved from Namibia to South Africa. He was in Hillbrow in Johannesburg plying his trade, his "docky business." I learnt that he finally travelled himself- to Europe to continue with his trade. That's how I travelled to Cameroon, and it was never discovered. They would always call me Anyu. I was bearing his name. My name became Anyu for the one month that I was in Cameroon, I became Anyu. I went to Cameroon-we had my mother's *crydie* and then I came back.

When I returned to Johannesburg, a big surprise awaited me. Tony Pereira was at the top of our organization. He was a shrewd and selfish Canadian who knew nothing about African culture and traditions. He was the one in charge of our company in South Africa. I told him that I was going for my mum's funeral and he asked me not to go, claiming that I had just opened an office that needed my full attention and presence. I said to him, "You are a Canadian you don't understand African Tradition. I must go. They have planned this funeral for a long time and I am the first born and chief celebrant, this lady died when I was en route to South Africa, and it is now more than a year since her death, how can I not go?" He still insisted I shouldn't go, but I had decided and so I went. When I left here I had saved R50,000 in less than six weeks, which meant my office was doing well, very well, compared to others. Others were not making that kind of money. There was no way that Tony was going to tell me that my office was not doing well. He couldn't say that, because the rule of the company is that you will go on retrain; your office will be closed down, only if you are not doing well. So when I came back from Cameroon I went to my manager's office, and was surprised to see four of my office staff at his office. I asked them what they were doing there. My promoting manager had come down to Cape Town, closed my office, and took the guys who were working with him back to Johannesburg.

My promoting manager, Kuze, it turned out, had been forced to do it. It was not his idea, it was Tony's. But he could not tell me, he had to save his face. He had to stand like the one in authority because he was my promoting manager. So when I went to his office and asked him what is happening he told me you have to come back on retrain. I asked him why. He said, "Your attitude, you don't have the right attitude, you need to go back on retrain. They asked you not to go to Cameroon and you defied orders and you went so that's why they've closed down your office."

I don't believe in these African traditional doctors and soothsayers, but something happened in Cameroon that makes me unsure of what to believe anymore. When I went on that trip for my mother's *crydie* –, family back home, they like those things –, and I arrived in Abakwa, the first thing that uncle Ni did was to force me to go with him to a traditional healer before I went home. He said the traditional healer had to work on me, to fortify me against evil forces at home, so to speak. So I reluctantly went with him and that healer said something. He told me, "You're going back to Cape Town, when you get back to South Africa, you will lose something, something very important to you. It is going to take you a long time to get it back." That's what he said, adding that there was nothing I could do about it. That's what the traditional doctor said and when I got here, my office was closed down.

Incidentally, I later on met this very same tradition healer in Cape Town. I was running an office in Salt River. This man came into my office through another Cameroonian in Parow. He wanted an employment letter to go and apply for permanent residence. He came, sat, just looking at me. He told me, "I know you, where do I know you from?" I said, "I've seen you but I don't remember..." that was after some time. Then I discovered that was the native doctor my uncle had taken me to see. He had followed me to Cape Town, the place he had rightly predicted I was going to lose something very important to me. Small world, this is! I helped him. We became very good friends. He plies his trade in South Africa, Cameroon and other African Countries. He hardly misses an occasion that involves me. He even attended my Dad's funeral and memorial back home each time with a contingent of friends with a carload of goodies and drinks. Doctor is my friend but I only used his services that one time, at the behest of Uncle Ni.

It took me some time to decide what to do. If I knew what I knew now, I wouldn't have gone back on retrain. I should have gone on my own because now I am on my own. It took me time to decide. Finally, I decided to go back. I left my family in that flat and I went back. I couldn't stop imagining the prospects of making R40,000 a month, I refused to see myself going back to the life of street hawking, pitching on the stands and hoping for the best. So I went back on retrain for one full year, twelve months. I had lost motivation, so it took me much longer than it would have had I been as zealous as before. All the months that I was on retrain I was just there. It was not a very good experience because I was leaving from a stage where I was making over R20,000 a month and going back to a situation where I had to make say R2000 a month. How much money I made was dependent on how much profit I made on my personal sales. It was very tough financially and emotionally. I don't want to believe what they said about my attitude, because I didn't believe that paying one's last respects to one's mother was having the wrong attitude. But they were in a position of force, and I could choose to comply or to perish as far as this business was concerned. At the time, I didn't know what I know today, and thought I desperately needed them to succeed.

It was during that time that my relationship with my wife deteriorated. We had a crisis. Staying away from your family for such a long time spelt trouble for my marriage. The money was not there to support them as my stands in Cape Town were not yielding much. When South Africans see something that is making money they want to own it. So those stands were closed in Cape Town, because South Africans started rioting. They went on the streets asking the municipality to take away the stands from foreigners and give to them. And because I was not there, that's what happened. They took away all the stands on The Parade in Cape Town. So I was not making money from the stands. They were all closed down. My wife was, at the time, still working with the security industry. She was not business minded. I never wanted her to do that security thing. I wanted her to join me, so that we could do this business together. Then when the time came she could go to school and fulfil herself, since that was something she wanted to do – higher education.

My wife was in Cape Town with the family and the kids. We had two more kids in Cape Town, all boys like Taanji. I guess that was also another problem. The money was not coming in as it used to and for such a long time. But all the same, while I was away, I did my best to look after my family in Cape Town. I did my best, but then, when I got promoted to a Manager again, my wife suggested, and we agreed that I should stay on in Johannesburg and open my office there, with the understanding that she would move with the family to Johannesburg and join me.

I opened my office in Braamfontein in Johannesburg and

she was supposed to come join me there with the kids. When I opened that office, I started making money again. I expected the family to come and meet me in Johannesburg, so I had to look for a bigger place. I expected her to come up to Johannesburg with the family, now that I had set up the office and was back in business. I told her to liquidate whatever she had in Cape Town because it was going to be very expensive to transport things to Johannesburg. She agreed. I took on a flat. I rented a 2 bedroom flat in Braamfontien. The flat belonged to a Cameroonian *feyman* – so we call a fraudster businessman back home – who suddenly ran out of money. It was very well equipped, it had everything and it was a very nice flat. The furniture inside was very good. So we agreed that I was going to take over the flat and pay for the furniture, pay for everything. I did that, and I moved into the flat. I was doing that because I knew my family was coming. But I did not tell my wife. I wanted it to be a surprise.

Finally when my wife came, it was not a good surprise for her. She had a surprise of her own for me. She had to return to Cape Town. I might not be able to go into the details here but the long and short of it is that it became too much. I loved my kids, I love my kids so very much I became a very unhappy person living away from them. I had been in Johannesburg for a total of about four years. I wanted to move back to Cape Town so as to be with my family. So I closed shop in Braamfontein and moved to Cape Town. It was a tough decision to make. But I had to do it.

But as much as I loved to be with my family under one roof, the damage had been done, and it was never to be the same again. I suppose my four years living in Johannesburg have put the death nail on my marriage. It's amazing that you can suffer together with somebody the way I did with my wife for so many years until 2003, then they turn their back on you in a way you cannot understand. The only reason I went to Johannesburg was because I loved my family so much I wanted a better life for them. It is the same reason I ever did anything in my life. I love family and I love to support people. But that again is a story better told another day.

When I left Cameroon, my wife and I were not actually married. We were engaged and she waited for me all that while. She waited for me for how many months? First, I left her in Cameroon and went to Saudi Arabia for six months. She waited for me. I came back to Cameroon and was there for about two years or less than that. Then I left again for South Africa and it took me sixteen months to get to South Africa, sixteen months during which she did not know if I was alive or dead. Then it took me another two years again, after I left Cameroon, to see her. And she was waiting for me all this while. The only reason I think she waited for me was because she loved me. It could not have been because of anything other than love. It wasn't anything else, it was love. I loved her too. I truly loved her. We loved each other so much that we were prepared to wait for each other for years; we were prepared to go against the wishes of our parents too. She rejected many suitors to be with me. I broke the hearts of a couple of ladies to be with her.

When I started to date this woman, I went through a lot. My father never wanted me to marry her. No family member wanted me to get married to her. Not because of her as a person, not even because of her family but because they wanted me as the first born in the family, to get married to someone from the village whom they know. It was that kind of a thing. It's not because they hated her, or had something against her. This is the woman I loved and we had a kid while we were still at university in Yaoundé. I didn't see why I shouldn't love the woman with whom I had a kid, but should leave her and get married to someone I didn't even know. She knew all that and she went through all that. The only person who supported me, not supported me as such but who said something like, "what makes you happy makes me happy", was my sweet mother, my late dear mother. I don't care where she comes from, she used to say. My mother used to be very dynamic and understanding. My mother didn't go to school, but she was much more intelligent in the things of life than some PhD holders in life and social sciences I know. That was the only consolation I had from the whole family. That's why my ex-wife, even till today, still regrets that my mother died. They loved each other a lot. Even her family, they loved my mother so much. It was only later on that we played a trick on my granddad. My granddad came to recognize her.

While still at university in Cameroon, granddad, who was actually my uncle, recognized this lady because of a trick I played with one of my cousins, Wopong. Wopong posed as this lady, and went to see my granddad. At the end of that visit my granddad was convinced that this was the lady, so thinking that my cousin was the woman I intended to marry, he said good, this lady is fine. So if you really insist, go for it. That was the second person, apart from my late mother, who gave me his blessings to marry the woman of my choice. My Dad then had to accept it because that was what made me happy. Because my Dad did not give his blessings to our relationship, I went for one full year without talking to him. I regret what I did then. He even had to travel the long distance to her village for the marriage rites.

The thing is, when two people get married the relationship transcends that of the duo. The families and friends get involved and the more so, especially when kids come into the picture. It becomes a life relationship even when the original two are no longer together. Ours was a chequered relationship of sorts from the beginning. Coming from different backgrounds and tribes, there was bound to be conflict and reluctance to accept the relationship from both sides. Her elder brother (whom we now affectionately call Brother) who never wanted to see me, being very protective of the sister, even right from the university days when they used to live in one room, eventually warmed up to me. We became very good friends so much so that he named his son James, after me and where I come from, that is humbling, a big honour. The aunty she grew up with, and many close relatives who were at first hostile towards our relationship, eventually embraced us. Her mother became my mother. She took the place of my mom especially when she passed away. I loved and cherished her love as a mother until she passed on. We all miss her. We were not getting along. But now, over ten years later, we get along. At least there's some level of understanding. We have to move on, but the family doesn't understand that. They are still very committed to the relationship; my relatives and hers alike.

At least for now, there's some understanding. We work together. We get along. The kids are with me. They have been living with me since 2003. They go to her most weekends and holidays when she's around. Her job is such that she moves around quite a bit. She is sometimes in Senegal, Ivory Coast, USA, and other countries. She runs an NGO. When you have kids living with another woman there is always a vacuum, but I love my kids and I love having them around. Taanji had long joined us in Cape Town, from Cameroon. He is now an adult studying in the university. But he lives with us.

My family life will never be normal like in a normal home. There'll always be problems here and there. I have accepted that. It is taking my kids a long time to adjust and understand that their mother could not live in the same house with them and their father. Kids will always want the parents to live together but they are gradually coming to terms with it. It will take some time. They say time heals all wounds.

I normally give my all in everything I do; not only in relationships. If I want to do something and I decide I want to do it I am going to give it a hundred and ten percent. But once there's a breach of trust, especially in a relationship; social, business or otherwise, it takes forever to repair. I've not actually repaired a breach of trust. It takes a long time for me to actually forget. When I went back to my first love, I was not really involved with the second one. When she breached the trust and I left her, I wanted to move on. Only circumstances brought her back to my life. I didn't go looking for her. She came looking for me. By that time I was already involved with someone. I don't want to betray people, so I made her understand I was with someone else.

Sma is the current woman in my life. I knew Sma in Johannesburg, but we were not involved then. We worked together, first when I was doing my training, and later as administrator in my office in Johannesburg. When I came down to Cape Town, there was no plan with her. It was only after my wife left me that I got involved with her. I don't want to betray people. I don't want to betray people's trust. When they betray me I feel really hurt. I don't easily forgive. It's not in my nature. I might forgive but I don't forget. There are certain things that you cannot repair. There are certain cracks in a relationship that are there for life.

Chapter 10

Life as an Immigrant Businessman in South Africa

The truth is revealed to people in degrees. If you are at home in the village what happens is you rely more on family. When you get out of the village, and move to town, you start opening up to other truths, you start having other friends, other acquaintances who are not family, people you don't know. And when you move to an even bigger town or city, you rely less and less on the family to get things done. You are less reliant on family and the more you depend on strangers, so much so that at one point you have yourself having a family of strangers.

I think it's just the way it is. When I left Cameroon, I left the whole family at home. The person I was with was just a friend at home, Anyu. Even though he then became like my family. But, there were so many other people who had a big influence in my life, people who helped me along the way, in one way or another, and those people were not family, they were total strangers.

I've come to realize that most people who have helped me in my life were strangers —strangers in the sense of not being blood relations. Apart from my immediate family, my mum and my dad and a few others – some brothers or sisters (direct siblings or cousins), a few uncles or aunties – the majority of the family, especially the extended relations are not interested in helping me. They are interested in milking me. From my experience, these strangers are not interested in giving to you. Rather they are interested in taking from you. But, you do come across a good number of total strangers who honestly go out of their way to help you without even knowing you or expecting a return of the favour. My journey from Cameroon to South Africa bares testimony to this fact. If I came all the way to South Africa, it was not because I knew anyone along the way. But I received a lot of support and help. I got financial, other material and moral support from people I did not even know.

The guy who lodged me for like twelve months, fed me, sometimes giving me pocket money, for instance, I never knew this man, and I have never seen him after the twelve months. It's close to twenty years today since I saw him. So, you find in life sometimes you can come across people who help you but who you will never see again. , Even if you wanted to pay them back, you don't have the opportunity to do that directly. Then it dawns on you that the only way of paying them back is continuing their good deeds by doing onto other perfect strangers what they did for you. You learn that one good turn deserves another, but not always or necessarily for those initially involved.

In Zaire, the Muslim community actually helped us, especially in Kinshasa. They believe in Islam that the more you give, the more you receive, and in each business it is compulsory that you pay your taxes, it is a gift to the poor, and it's called Zarka. It is just like in the Christian church, where you are encouraged to pay your tithes. In Islam, Zarka is more with giving to the poor. We benefited a lot from these people. There were people who were giving us a hundred dollars, two hundred dollars, the Zaire at the time was like the Rand today, a local currency. But Mombutu's currency was not strong enough, so they relied more on foreign currency like the dollar. The Franc CFA was more respected in Zaire than the local currency.

I came to realize something else. The fact that I became

Muslim actually facilitated things for me. I have realized that Islam is a religion where they encourage giving and helping people. No matter what people say about Islam, Islam is a great religion. The only reason why I changed again to Christianity was because of fellowship. In my family I was the only Muslim and my kids were practicing Christian, my wife is a Christian, my mother and father were all Christian, and so I just thought that it was going to be easier to create a better family for me if we could fellowship together. That's why I changed. Islam is a great religion. If you have gone through the experiences that I went through, you will see this clearly. All through our journey the majority of the people who helped us financially, morally and materially were Muslims. They were all Muslims.

The Islam that is practiced in the rest of Africa is different from the one that is practiced here in South Africa. Islam in the rest of Africa is much purer than here. There are lots of impurities in the version practiced here in South Africa. It is different, very different. Otherwise, Islam everywhere is a helping religion. Islam encourages you to help someone who is in need. It doesn't matter where you come from, it doesn't matter whether you're Christian or Muslim, it doesn't matter – as long as he is in need, help him. Christianity has got a lot of good principles, but they don't practice it. The majority of Christians don't practice. Islam has good principles and they put them into practice. That's the difference between the two. A lot of people helped me along the way, but what comes to mind is that Islam actually helped me a lot. The fact that I was Muslim opened many doors for me. Even my friend, Anyu, with whom I travelled to South Africa, left Cameroon as a Christian, but ultimately he was converted to Islam in Zaire. He remains a Muslim. A very striking observation again is that when you take the kind of journey that we undertook, you come across a lot of people, a lot also going your route. I discovered that the majority of the Christian, the majority of the people who set off on the journey to South Africa or wherever as Christian, ended up arriving as Muslims.

Predominantly, the hustler uses anything he can to convert to Muslims because they want to be accepted. Generally, they want to be supported and they want to get ahead and that's why I said some of them, when they get to their destination, they revert back to their original religion. Sometimes it's too late, because when they do that they also change their documents. I know a Cameroonian who today is known as Abubakar, his residence permit in South Africa has his name as Abubakar, but when you look at his certificates from home, it's a different name altogether. Back home they don't know him as Abubakar. Even here, I'm tempted to believe that his wife and kids do not know his real Cameroonian name.

The docky doctors are at the heart of this. They are identity converters. They are like dealers in currencies, bureau de change, in a way. You come in and you say I want to buy Cameroonian certificates, and a docky doctor gives them to you. I want to buy South African identities, he gives them to you. Such a person is known here as the Minister of Home Affairs. They can produce or fake any document that you want. Sometimes what they fake is better than the original. There have been instances where the fake documents are taken as the authentic and those with the originals are accused of being fakes.

The Cameroonian driving license is a good example. Because the South African traffic police are so used to the fake, they are likely to detain the few drivers with the authentic license for driving with fake licenses. The Cameroonian drivers' license produced by the docky doctors here is best used in the confines of South Africa. I went to Cameroon and I forgot that that was a fake license. It slipped my mind that I don't have to use that license in Cameroon. There was this night when I was driving confidently around my neighbourhood in Cameroon when I was stopped by the police. They asked for my license. I took it out with confidence, and handed it to the policeman. He took one look at it and asked me to park my car and step out. They told me that I must lead them to the manufacturer of this license that there are a lot of them around and they know that these are manufactured in Yaoundé, Douala and Mutenguene. They wanted to know where I had made mine. The long and short of the story is that I had to bribe my way out of that situation. I lost 10,000 francs there. I've had experiences with my drivers' license in Cameroon. Since the incident with the fake license in Cameroon, I always drive with a certificate of missing documents whenever I get back home until I obtained the legal driver's license. But, like most others, I keep both as I need the fake one in South Africa.

The docky doctors are amazing, very talented. I used to think a docky doctor is a negative element in the society, but given the circumstances, given the surroundings that we sometimes find ourselves in, he is actually very helpful. Most of the students from Africa, be it Nigeria, Cameroon, or wherever, who excel in schools in South Africa – they even come out with distinctions –, wouldn't have got their admission without the help of docky doctors. Most of them will tell you that if they are honest. It's the docky doctor who had to come out with a good result slip and all the documents that they need and the grades that they need, for them to go and get admission, and when they get it, they go and excel. That shows you that the system of education of Cameroon or Nigeria or Ghana or whatever country they come from in Africa is not as bad as people think it is.

Docky doctors make students very resourceful and work harder. And with that spirit, they get out of Cameroon and they excel. One of the first African immigrants to have done Nursing in South Africa came from an arts background. He had GCE A Level in Arts, English literature and whatever, but thanks to the docky doctor, who came up with the required certificates, she got admitted to do Nursing at a renowned university and he was one of the best. He was the one who opened the way at that university for African immigrants. So whenever you come to study Nursing at most South African universities, they say you are good. He didn't even know what biology was all about prior to registration to do the programme, but he excelled. So docky doctors have actually helped a lot of people.

Few are those who approach these docky doctors for papers and then cannot perform once they have been given a chance. The majority of those who use such certificates are people who are educated, but they don't have the required grades to get admitted, or those who have lost their certificates.

Docky doctors do everything. It's not just school certificates that they do. If you want pay slips, they will give them to you, if you want a tax certificate, visa related documents etc., they will give them to you. Just tell them whatever you want and they will deliver. If you've got a sample of what you need, they will make it for you. It's amazingly facilitating. They produce for you whatever you want. They have got a reservoir of assorted stamps and seals which they draw upon as need be. This trade has become so popular even amongst South Africans. The use of docky doctors is now not restrictive. South Africans and non-South Africans generally use their services. I hear it is popular everywhere, even out of South Africa; Europe, America, etc. It becomes cheaper for you, effortlessly cheaper. That's the magic of the fake. Docky doctors are facilitators. They have learnt to humble the world of bureaucracy and its infinite celebration of documented evidence.

Docky doctors have served as a nursery for the growing community of African immigrants in South Africa. When the community was small, the few Cameroonians who were here in Cape Town initially, we knew ourselves, and have remained more or less in contact, making an effort to meet every now and again, even if only to have a meal or to share a drink. But when the community started growing bigger and bigger with the assistance of docky doctors, one couldn't keep pace with everyone who passes for a Cameroonian. The result has been for me to pick and choose those I relate to on a regular basis, over and above the Pinyin community with whom I have regular events and engagements concerning development initiatives back home.

I have a friend in Johannesburg, Mukam, who is like a brother to me as well. We have come a long way. He's the one I left in Victoria to collect money for the car that I sold but had to leave before it was fully paid for. We are in the same business today. He came to South Africa because of me, but he decided to stay on in Johannesburg while I came to Cape Town. I trained him in my business and promoted him to a manager. We ran an office in Johannesburg together then I left him there and came down here. We are still very good friends, he's like family now. I talk to the wife every now and then. Mukam has been here for more than twelve years, getting to fourteen years and has never seen the wife. He left his wife in Cameroon when he travelled to South Africa. Later his wife won the American lottery. They agreed that his wife should proceed to the US. She went to the US. She's been there now for about eight years and they have never seen each other. Mukam would go home and see the kids regularly. The kids stayed in Victoria. They talk on the phone regularly. The wife was even operated upon a couple of days back. I spoke to her the other day. She finally got a green card after such a long struggle. I know her to be a good woman. It must be terribly difficult for both of them to stay apart for such a long time. But I believe with the wife getting the green card, it would be much easier for them to come together again. I keep wondering what is the essence of winning the American Lottery if one still has to take so long a time to get a green card, to obtain the right to live and work in America? Is it not supposed to be automatic? Why would winners of the Lottery go through such a cumbersome and costly procedure, pay their own flights from their countries of origin, and still face such difficulties to settle in Uncle Sam's Land of milk and honey? I know of a friend, a winner of the said Lottery, who has been in the US for over fourteen years but still hasn't got documents to work or travel to his home country. He lost his father long ago and has not been able to go home since. Another one had to travel on a different passport through a neighbouring country only to bury his dead mother at home. Like many of us, he is one of those in the diaspora with multiple identities that do not always complement one another. I know both Mukam and his wife always wanted the kids to go to the US and stay with their mother. And thank goodness they now have technologies such as smartphones and iPads equipped with Skype and webcams to facilitate long distance relationships.

Few of those that I knew a long time ago here in South Africa have been stagnant. There have been changes, positive changes. You only come across a few cases of negative changes or stagnation. When I look back, Sango my friend, he's a doctor now, PhD, but when I met him we were all on the stands together. He had come to Cape Town from Cameroon through Botswana, with a background in law, just like me. Sango introduced me to some very responsible Cameroonians in the academic field including some of my very learned friends at several prominent universities in South Africa. One of them recently graduated with a PhD from a university in Europe. Her thesis involved something on bushfallers and communication with Pinyin and Mankon as case studies. It was my pleasure to let her use my compound in Payak City as her base while doing her research in Pinyin. She and her husband live in their lovely home in Cape Town and own many properties in Cameroon and other countries. Anyu is working with the Cape Town Municipality as one of the Directors, he's got a good job now. He had earlier worked for Shoprite in Cape Town, the South African Revenue Services (SARS) in the customs department in Musina and with the Western Cape Parliament- all managerial positions. He's got a couple of properties in Cape Town. Sango is staying in his own house, and has constructed a big student hostel back in Buea, Cameroon, in addition to having a well-paying job with the Research Office of the University of Cape Town. My family members have grown. My kid brother has got a good job. He's got some properties in Cape Town and back home he drives a nice car in Cameroon. The one in Pretoria as well; he has a house at home and is doing well here. Ndoda, my brother in Johannesburg is just so good in what he does. He is very successful. He's invested a lot in properties both at home and in Jozi as well. I remember when he abandoned his job as HOD in GHS Nkambe, being a category A2 teacher from the Higher Teachers' Training School in Yaoundé, to follow me to South Africa. Many thought he was mad to resign from such a good job government job. But today Ndoda is envied by those same people. I trained him in the Benoni office and he later on got promoted to a manager. We went through tough times together. I recall when his wife, Mengi, came in from Cameroon, we were both sleeping on a small lean mattress in a small room in Benoni and I taught her how to prepare our staple food then; spaghetti with one egg or with a small tin fish when we made a bit of money on the field. This was the food she cooked for us every day that we can afford to buy any food. We later moved to Braamfontein to start an office together and we could only then afford a single room in which three of us still slept on our lean mattress for a while. Mengi regretted on several occasions why she came to South Africa. Today, that's a thing of the past as she and her husband have become very successful in their different businesses and also as a family. Indeed, Ndoda has been pillar of support to me in more ways than one. In different ways people have grown and are reaping the rewards of the daring mobility that brought them to South Africa.

I've got a couple of friends who are non-Cameroonians and non-South Africans. Most of these friends are friends I met when we came to South Africa in 1995. I think at that time there were very few foreigners, so we were bound to be close. The few foreigners that were here, especially West Africans, we identified with each other. I am still in touch with a couple of friends, mostly Nigerians. I had a Ghanaian friend who apparently left the country. I don't know where he is now. One of my best Nigerian friends Akim that I met in Namibia on my way to South Africa was here for a while. He left for Australia with his South African wife. I remember him as being the first foreigner to invite me to a party in Khayelitsha, to celebrate his wedding, where the music of the late Brenda Fassie was prominent. I was honoured with the Master of Ceremonies. I didn't know I was a man of many talents. I made such a good MC that after that, most people who were present, immigrants and South Africans alike would only call me Mr MC. I also got plenty of other invites to be MC in subsequent occasions. That was a long time ago. We communicated for some time but I lost contact with him. I last spoke with him when he was thinking of going to Britain after barely two years in Australia. He used to be an IT technician in those pre-cell phone days, and was famous among his foreigner friends for his regular alerts on what public telephone booth was not working properly so they could flock there to make free calls.

Sam, the Nigerian that I crossed from Namibia to South Africa with, is still very much a friend. We visit each other and when we got here we were eventually doing the same thing in terms of business, we all had stands on the parade in Cape Town. Now, most of my friends are not that close. We are scattered and have moved from the lines of business we used to do in those days. We just meet once a while, and with the advent of the cell phone we are able to have regular conversations over long distances. I may not go to Johannesburg or Pretoria or Durban often, but I am able to reach out to my friends in these places with the help of the cell phone. Quite a few friends have left the country, friends of old, I think most of them have left the country. Once in a while you find a friend coming in from Australia, Britain, from the US and we still meet, but I would not say those are serious relationships. I had a couple of friends from Kenya, from Tanzanian, Algeria, even Libya and from elsewhere as well, brought together in those days as having in common the status of being foreigners in South Africa. We happened to be doing the same thing in those days, sometimes staying together.

There is Kuze, my trainer and manager with whom I used to work in the Canadian DS Max company. We became very good friends, especially after he invited me to join him in his new Johannesburg office. But then, you cannot be very good friends with your boss for too long. When people get rich, they usually change their friends as well, but that is not the case with us. It's just that I discovered along the line that my boss was just like a Jew, a Shylock. He makes friends with you because he knows he's going to make money from you and when that doesn't happen, the friendship suffers. Now we're not very good friends anymore because we both changed divisions I DS Max. It's about four years since I've seen him, a very long time. But we were very good friends, so much so more that I knew about him intimately. He's quite a character. He's someone that you would like to know. I like his business mind. This is that kind of person who wants things and means it. Kuze is that kind of a person who says I want this done and it's done.

I don't know how to describe this guy. He's a good character, he's got different sides but the one thing that I don't see in Kuze is a family man. He's not a family man. He will move from one woman to the next, just like that. And he makes a lot of money. He's that kind of a person when he wants to make money he makes it and when he makes money he also squanders it. That's Kuze. He will drive flashy cars and virtually it is because of that that I got attracted to investments. I guess I wanted to be different from Kuze. I discovered that if you don't make money you cannot spend the way you're spending. Kuze made so much money while I was with him, I was actually thinking that he should have invested a lot of money, but there was no investment.

Kuze rented a flat and lied to us that he bought it, only for us to discover he didn't buy the flat. When he moved out, someone else moved in, and the landlord came around to sign a new lease agreement with the new tenant. He likes money so much that he will do anything for money. He doesn't care whether you're his friend or his brother or sister; as far as money is concerned. He's got no conscience with money. Kuze goes to extra lengths to make money. At one time he bought a bakkie and was using that vehicle to go to the field to transport workers and things like that. I was running an office in Braamfontein. He was in Benoni. He came with the car to my office. Then he parked his bakkie in the parking lot, came to my office and was with me for about two hours or so. We went out, each time I saw him check his phone and his watch. Then I started asking myself what was going on. I asked him why he was so itchy. He told me he was waiting for a call, a very important call from a friend who was coming in from somewhere. That was not true. He was waiting for a call quite alright, but not from a friend.

After some time Kuze received a call. It was not a call but a beep. Then I saw how he jumped up. I walked him out, and when we got to the parking lot for him to drive off, his car was not there. He pretended he didn't know where the car had gone. We searched and searched and searched and, instead of reporting the missing car immediately, he took me to a restaurant, where we ate, had a drink and sat conversing. He was showing no signs of frustration for losing his car. I, on the other hand, was worried for him, as I thought time was running out for him to report the missing car. He only reported his car was missing after about four hours. When we got back to my office he called the police, called his insurance, to say his car had been stolen. That car was never found and the insurance paid and he never used to pay insurance for that car. He had taken up insurance for the car only two months back.

The first car that he bought was a BMW. He drove that car, came back to say that he was hijacked, and the story just ended like that. Insurance paid for the BMW, just as the insurance paid for the stolen bakkie.

I discovered afterwards that Kuze was playing games. He was stealing his own cars. He was organizing so that his own car should be stolen because you cannot come and tell me that you were hijacked at gun point and there's nothing wrong with you, no panic, nothing. I was close to him. So that's the kind of person he was. That's the kind of person Kuze was. He had a girlfriend he called his childhood friend, in Durban. When I met this girl, I discovered that Kuze was not a South African as he had claimed. He was actually a Zimbabwean. He was telling us one story about his origins and childhood and the girlfriend was telling us a different story. I happened to be friends with this lady through Kuze, so sometimes we would sit and chat then she would talk about their days in Zimbabwe when they were growing up, while Kuze would talk about their days in Durban when they were growing up. Kuze had actually formulated a story of this land and planned it so well and was selling it to people. He looks like that kind of Zimbabwean who came into the country a long time ago and obtained South African citizenship. He had an ID and things like that. He is sharp. He speaks almost all the languages in South Africa. Zimbabweans are sharp. He is always on his guard. But sometimes, even for a self-conscious person like Kuze, the Zimbabwean accent comes through. But most of the time, he ensures that he is seen and treated as South African. Kuze has used a lot of people that I know, including me, to make money. Kuze was out to make money, he didn't care about anyone. He just cared about himself. People like Kuze are always rich because they don't care. They want to make money at all cost.

My connection with South Africans is mostly in working relationships. The majority of South Africans that I have been friends with have been business partners. The one thing I have discovered with South Africans both black and white is that they remain your friends when they know that they are benefiting from you, especially the whites. I have been friends with a cross section of them and we became friends because of the business. That is actually my observation. They will kiss you. They will pamper you. They will do whatever to make you happy when they know they are benefiting from you. That is what I have discovered from my experience with South Africans.

I have also come across a few true South African friends. But the majority of South Africans that I have come across that I have been dealing with are basically from the work place. Maybe that is understandable, because we came to know each other from work related issues. It was just a working relationship. Maybe I mistook it for friendship. The majority of South Africans that I have worked with, they would hold out to be your friends when they are benefiting from you. When that changes, they are not friends anymore. I have seen that a lot in the line of business I work. I've worked with a lot of South Africans, so much so that, at one time, I discovered that it was not a good thing to bring those ones that you work with too close, because they are the same ones who will stab you in the back. They will steal from you. I had that experience in the previous company I worked with, in fact, all the companies I have been working with, beginning with Kuze and his promotion at the time when we first became very good friends. All he wanted was for us to work hard so he could make money.

There is Tony as well, whom I have referred to already. Tony was originally Canadian. He got married to a South African, so he became one with dual nationality. I suppose Canadian and South African laws permit dual nationality, just like most civilized nations of the world, unlike Cameroonian law that doesn't. As a Cameroonian, if you took on another nationality, you and your family automatically ceased from being a Cameroonian citizen. This is the case with many ordinary Cameroonians like my friend Anyu and my brother Ndoda. You will then need a visa to go to your own country. And while in Cameroon you will be treated as a foreigner in your land of birth. You will then resort to playing games the

Camer way to get any document like birth certificate and Cameroon ID that will enable you do things like open bank accounts, take loans or even invest in your own country. But as with many other laws in Cameroon, this law has a selective application. There are many Cameroonians on whom this law has no application like those in power, men of influence, with their relatives. These are those who consider themselves above the law. This explains why a bar examination can be annulled retroactively for some candidates like me and not for others like my university mate Mbia. This is the reason some of my mates and I are not practicing lawyers in Cameroon today, a profession we really cherished. Tony was my up line and he was just like a Jew. He promoted Joachim De Paolo, Kuze's promoting manager and Kuze promoted me, in DS Max International. He would make you work your ass off only for him to get what he wanted from you. This is the guy who, when I went home after my promotion to manager, for my mother's funeral, reprimanded me harshly for daring to do so. He said I had just opened an office and I had no right to leave and go to Cameroon. But I said this was my mother we were talking about and this is something that has been scheduled for a long time, then I went to Cameroon. When I came back Tony put me on *retrain*, closed my office, took me back to Johannesburg where I was on retrain basically, not making money for one year. This eventually cost me my marriage. Why did he do that? He wanted to take over my office in conspiracy with Kuze, so as to make more money, and to get back to me for standing up to him. They succeeded.

In South Africa business is a big mafia. I don't know whether it is the kind of business I got involved with, but a big mafia is the right description. It is not just because I am Cameroonian, even though it shows in most circumstances. Most businessmen in South Africa that I've come across have one underlining principle: they use people to make money. That's why they fail. Business pride thrives on people. I know that to make money, to sustain your business, you must have a rapport with people. But this 'mafia' don't understand that. All of the companies that I am talking about were only using people to make money. You can fool some people some of the time, as Bob Marley says! You can fool some people all the time but you cannot fool all the people all the time. It always comes out. And when it comes out they leave you. No one wants to spend their life just working for someone else, with no future prospects.

And when they leave you, what happens? The business crumbles. Most of the guys I am talking about today are not rich, like the recent one, Zack of Med-care 24. This guy is troubling. He had hired a Cameroonian. Then, this Cameroonian pitched us to go over to his company because he was using us as well. We went over; all of us. I went over with my managers, because I know I am good in what I do. I am good at building managers. I am good at keeping people motivated. That I am good at; that is what I do to make money. So when I moved over to Med-care 24. I went over with my managers - who numbered five at the time. We then met three more managers in the other company. Zack made a white guy president of the company, not on merit. At the first meeting we had with this guy, Zack, founder of Med-care 24, he was driving a very old car. That was in 2002, a very old BMW. I know that to suggest that someone with a BMW, no matter how old, is poor sounds contradictory, but truth be told: he was poor. He never had money. So when I walked into that meeting they explained to us – me and Mukam one of my managers - what they were doing. I understood it because we were in the same line of business.

I told them what I thought we should do if we were going

to work together. As I started setting goals, I told them the number of paying clients we were going to put into the system, for instance, the number of managers the company was going to have in one year, and so on and so forth. In hearing me say these things this guy almost collapsed. He asked me if I was sure of what I was saying. I said I was sure. He did not believe me. In just one year we achieved all the goals I had set., They were goals that the company had not achieved in the past three years. They had never achieved even a tenth of those goals. So I can say that me and my team basically built that company. We met the company with three managers. We built that company to 64 managers from 2003. I joined the company at the end of 2002. From then to end of 2007, we were 64 managers. And out of these 64 managers, 52 were down line managers in my organisation and the rest of them were from the other three managers. That's how much the company grew with my input. . I have developed a talent for people, peoples' skills. I never knew I possessed this talent.

When we arrived, the company's turnover was less than R200,000 a month. In 2007, the turnover of the company was R6,000,000 a month. Imagine less than R200,000 to R6,000,000 and that was in five years.

Suddenly, money got to Zack's head however, and he started buying cars left, right and centre. He had money. He had five private cars, including the BMW 330 series which had just come out. He bought a brand new one, he bought a Land Rover Discovery, he bought a sports car, he bought a building in Johannesburg, and another in Durban. He also bought private residences in these cities. He went to exotic holiday destinations with different women. You name them. He had grown from rags to riches. He had so much money he did not know what to do with it. It went into his head literally speaking, so much so that he started forgetting where all of it came from.

As for me, I bought all the properties I have during that time. I was making quite some money. That's the one thing that I achieved while working in that company. Zack did not want me to invest in property. He did not want me to do anything else apart from the business. He did not want any manager to do anything else. So I had to buy my properties behind his back. He did not know about it and when he found out he was furious. I became the black sheep instead of the hero of the company. He accused me of doing other business. But how can I be making money and I not invest? I am making money for you, you invest the money, but I have got my own money – I was making money, there was no lie about it – and you don't want me to invest? You want me to spend my money, waste all of it away, on cars and women like you? The politics there is that he wanted me to stay poor so that I had to stay glued to him. That is the philosophy that the other company had. It was even worse in the other company. They also wanted you to stay poor so that you would have to stay with them. I did not understand why it became a problem for someone to hear that I had bought a house with my own money, duly and immaculately earned. Then I came to understand that they were envious of the independence and self-assertion that that would bring me.

They want you to stay, immobilized. They hate anything that moves. When you are moving, making an effort, a move that is not engineered by them, they are very uncomfortable. They want to control you. That is exactly what I discovered. I don't understand why, if I am making money, you frown upon me when I invest it the way I like on what I like. Don't I have the right to do what I want to do with my own money? They wanted me to spend my money on wasteful expenditure. If I had come to the office boasting that I had thirteen girlfriends and all of them had gone shopping at Woolworths, Lewis, Edgars or whatever, he would have been very happy, and would have encouraged me to buy fancy cars for each of them as well as for myself. That's exactly what they were doing. They encouraged us to grace the shops with our earnings. They encouraged us to consume even before we had earned. The whole economy hates anybody who buys and pays cash. Such people are thought to be very dangerous to the economy, because it means that you can afford to think for yourself, and to go for what you need and not what you want.

That's exactly what these guys were doing. In the other company, the founder of the company came up with a policy that he was going to buy cars for all managers. We thought it was a bonus for working hard. But that was not what they had in mind. The idea was for them to pre-finance the purchase of those cars, and then start deducting the money from our earnings. In addition, we were to use the bakkies to make even more money for them. I left that place having paid more than two years of hired purchase and I did not have the car. It was mine only in principle. They organized training seminars and team building holidays in exotic venues across the country, even out of the country. But they debit the managers who had no say in these things in the first place. In these companies, you don't earn a salary. You earn your own income by working hard, putting the work into it. So you can earn as much as you want. They say you run your own franchise, your own office or company, but they control you, they control your money. So they can do what they want with your money. They always want to do things that will keep you poor, keep you working for them. They hate independent thinkers. That is just how they operate.

So when this guy saw me buying a car with cash, instead of me going to take accounts at shops, , he felt violated – the very principles around which he constituted his life had crumbled. Even worse, he discovered that most of the houses I had bought were not mine to live in. Instead, they were generating income, because I was renting them out. Here was a baby running even before it had been allowed to walk, he must have thought. He got pissed off. I used to teach financial planning to all of my managers. During one seminar we had towards Lesotho, in the Drakensberg, I was supposed to deliver a paper on financial planning, but this guy told me that I must only talk about how people push to make money and to work hard and invest in their businesses. I must have left the people with an unanswered question: what do you do with the money earned? That is the question they don't want people asking, let alone answering. I felt uncomfortable not telling them the whole truth. So, during the lunch break, I sat with most of the participants on the same table and took the opportunity to tell them that someone who makes R100,000 a month and squanders R90,000 a month on himself or other things is worse off than somebody who does not even make R1,000. I encouraged them to save their money, to avoid debt, or to pay it off as quickly as possible, and to buy with cash. When this guy discovered what I had done, despite his efforts to stop me, he was furious.

That's why they hire and fire - they know those two words very well. Nobody dares last long enough to discover the secret of the firm, except the person that founded it or is a very close ally. The whole notion of the contract entails that they hire and fire on a regular basis in order to show that they are always the ones in charge. You're never comfortable enough to be able to plan things differently or even say what you think about the way things are run. I found an issue with the system. They want you to be indebted, and the whole idea is because, you see, in the days of apartheid it was a mechanism for the whites to make money, since they owned all the shops, all the economy, it was a big way for them to make money, you buy something for R1,000 and in 24 months you are going to pay R4,000. It's even better. They know how to protect themselves. You are encouraged to pay taxes on almost everything you make except what you make from shares in South Africa. Shares are exempted from taxes. Why would that be when only an elite few can afford to make enough money to think of buying shares in a company? Why would shares be exempt? They know people who can save up enough to buy them. The ordinary person who saves even a little thing, they tax him on interest which basically discourages the black and coloured people from ever saving at all. What is the point of saving when your savings will eventually be cut as taxes? Then those who can venture into property and shares are not taxed, and, to cover up their lame excuse, they say that they want to encourage investment. If you really want to encourage investment, start by encouraging savings, so that the person who earns less than a certain amount a year will not pay tax, increase the tax-free threshold on earnings. They could also encourage people who save R50,000, or less, a year by exempting them from tax on the interest they make. Then you will begin to see that people will be encouraged to save.

All they know to do towards the poor and miserable is to encourage them to take up funeral schemes. They want the poor to contribute their widow's mite on a monthly basis so that when they pass away, they will be buried in dignity. Why on earth should I stomach a life of misery in exchange for a dignified burial? Who cares? And to imagine that it is the very people who don't care whether or not I live a life worth living that are pretending to care that I am well buried after death, is the greatest hypocrisy I have experienced since coming to South Africa. Elsewhere in Cameroon we don't save away to bury the dead. We know that the community will come out in their numbers to make sure that even a homeless person who dies is given a good burial. In South Africa, and elsewhere out of Cameroon, most Cameroonians don't pay for funeral schemes. But I don't remember any Cameroonian corpse that was not repatriated home and given a decent and dignified burial. All funerals are dignified funerals whether or not you are buried by family or by strangers, because the sight of an abandoned corpse is a sign of our collective failure as a society. So I challenge all these companies to prove that they care by actually taking care of the living and not by preying on their fears to defraud them of the peanuts they earn in this life with dubious funeral schemes.

In this last company the financial crunch actually affected us. That's where the biggest problem came. We were actually in the financial industry and we made money from debit orders from the banks. And when the economic crisis set in our income started going down, it would not have been bad if the founder of the company did not implement certain bad measures. Between 2006 and 2008 was that I was at the peak of my earnings, but towards the end of 2008 things started going bad and my income from the company started falling at an alarming rate. It continued falling, falling, and falling until I left in 2010. At the beginning of 2010, I was making barely a third of my 2008 earnings and there was no prospect in sight. There was no hope of our company picking up. The founder of the company was in debt. He had taken so much. He bought a building in Johannesburg for the head office, another in Durban, he had a block of flats, in Johannesburg, he had his personal residence in Johannesburg, he had his personal residence in Durban, and about four more properties in Durban, and so forth. Most if not all of these were bonded properties. There were all those cars that he was servicing too.

When the going was good there was no problem. But, as my income fell by over seventy percent, the income of the company fell too because I was the main player. So, with this guy's income falling, how was he going to take care of all those debts that he owed?

There was no other way apart from cheating us. That is what killed the company. I discovered that he had stolen a lot of money from us, a lot! It was the same thing with the other company, Premier Growth, even though the atmosphere or economic climate at the time was different. But I have come to learn this about some people: when they get rich, they want to continue getting richer at all cost, even at the cost of the less rich. It is called greed, the green eyed monster, it drives the capitalist world where the rich get richer, by depraving the less rich, and the poor get poorer. But, like the law of gravity that never fails, when you cheat the less fortunate out of what is theirs, natural justice always comes to their aid. What goes around comes around. You pay for your sins often times even here on earth. Most people discovered it so everyone started leaving. The banks repossessed most of his houses and the cars were auctioned off. That was a case of a giant fall. It was a big fall but it was not supposed to be like that if he had invested in people, if he had put people first, if he had invested wisely. Like others I lost my income, hard earned earnings that I spent several years building up, but, thankfully, I did not lose any one of my houses. I did not lose any property. In fact, my properties became my major source of income.

Zack was a white South African. If he had cared to listen to me, I would have told him that I would not take a bond and buy a house, and that I will always seek to pay from my pocket first, and only take a supplementary bond if absolutely necessary. Even if I buy a house with a hundred percent bond, that house must be able to pay for the bond itself. I would only buy a property with potential, a property that I can renovate, or add more value to it in order that it manages to pay for itself. I don't think he would have listened - he clearly loved the good life too much. To him, any advice I volunteered would have sounded like the irritation of a thousand vuvuzelas at a Kaizer Chiefs and Orlando Pirates soccer showdown. He wanted to be a big man who buys a big mansion and takes his daughter to stay there, and buys another big property, and this one is only used for holidays. He wanted to hire gardeners and maintenance workers, in addition to security guards, he wanted to go to casinos in Sun City with a band of young blood suckers called ladies, and to Zanzibar and Mauritius with different women on holidays, all as evidence of his being a big man. To him, he was selling the image of the business. He called it promoting or publicity.

I've worked with a lot of South Africans. In my business, we take people with matric or in those days standard eight, and train them. So we are dealing with the common man, not with the very educated people. I am pleased things picked up again for me, and that working for myself is paying off. But I am not yet there. I haven't arrived quite yet.

Presently, I've got 71 people in total in my location, my own company, Premier Attraction cc, not a franchise. I have so far promoted five managers. I intend to promote more. My passion is to work with young people, groom them in the business from nothing to something and to give them and their families a future. We are growing big time. We've seen that kind of growth in a very short time. God is hearing my prayers, I must say. My greatest problem now is that of capital. I didn't plan for this growth and now that there is growth it means that the capital that I use for merchandise, I need to step it up. I am getting there. I am running out of space. I have been asking the owner of my building to give notice to some of his tenants so I could take over more space in the building. I am not so happy because the tenants don't want to move, and when you start growing like that you can grow more. I just discovered last week that I am actually running out of space. But we will sort that out. Maybe look for some new premises, if this does not work out.

Out of about seventy people in the office almost all of them are South Africans, and just one or two of them achieved some kind of a diploma after matric. The rest of them are at the level of grade ten, grade eleven, or matric. So those are the kind of people I am dealing with. That is how the business has been ever since I joined the business. The kind of South Africans that I interact with are people that need to be groomed. They come mostly from the locations (townships), they come from school, and most of them know very little about life. But we groom them and train them. Once in a while you will find others who have experience in life, but they are the minority.

My impression of South Africans in relation to those that I have been working with is that they are terribly conscious of the discrimination they suffered under apartheid, and that if they appear lazy it is more because they crave for restitution and entitlements. It is not laziness as I know it within my own family and among Cameroonians, for example. I would hardly ever claim that Cameroonians work harder than South Africans. But South Africans feel, and perhaps rightly so, that they don't have to work too hard to make ends meet. And why should they? After all, most of them or their parents and departed loved ones have sweated and spilled blood for decades and had nothing but misery and the deep resilient wounds of racism to show for it., Cameroonians and West Africans on the other hand have a strong entrepreneurial spirit that many South Africans don't have. South Africans must work for other people, perhaps because apartheid made them to perpetually present themselves as dependent children, even to those who were clearly physically and intellectually under-qualified to boss over them. The scars of a past of unequal encounters and continual debasement are as stubborn as hell. My business is the kind of business where we don't want you to work for us. We want you to work for yourself. That is the whole logic. So that explains why most of the time it is so difficult for us to grow. Most of the people that come to look for jobs look for jobs where they will earn R1,500 – R2,000 – R3,000. They are minimalists and don't actually believe that they can achieve much more in their lives. When they come and you start telling them that you are going to make them manager – a manager makes plus minus R20,000 a month –, to them this is scary. Too much money! To them that is too much money and it is impossible to make that kind of money. That is how limited they are in their reasoning. So most of the time, the people that we hire, that we train, they are that low in their ambitions. I remember this lady, Bongi, in my office. When I asked her about her goals and when she was going to buy her car, in awe she told me something like: "Jib, buy a car? No I don't want to buy a car. Why Bongi?" I asked, she replied, "How can I buy a car? No one in my whole family ever owned a bicycle, so how can I buy a car, Jib?" Apartheid was savage in the way it has deprived many South Africans of self-worth and ambition.

At the end of the day, maybe out of thirty people, only one will make it and become a manager. And when that one becomes a manager he makes money. But, even when they start making money they don't want to work. That is the problem. It would appear that when they make money they just want to go and spend all the money. And then they settle for just going back to work. In this fashion, they never save. They buy things on hire purchase: hire purchase on cars, hire purchase on furniture, hire purchase on clothing, hire purchase on this and that. And they end up paying ten times more and it becomes a spiral kind of thing. It goes round and round and round. And who owns the shops where they queue up for hire purchase? The same people who owned the shops prior to 1994, the purported year when apartheid is supposed to have ended.

I read a book titled *"The Capitalist Nigger"*, by a Nigerian in the US. When I read that book it changed my mentality. I have a personal copy which I take with me everywhere I go. When I read that book it changed my way of reasoning and I find fault with South Africans because they keep on recycling the poverty cycle. It goes round and round. It is like a cycle that never ends. There is something we call in our business the law of averages. It is like a revolving door. Take a revolving door when people go in, they come out. When a lot of people go into a business a few will do business with you and a lot of them will also come out. In South Africa, the majority of the people who go in through that revolving door always come out. Very few of them will stay. In my business, I might have these seventy one people that I am talking about. Out of these 71 people, maybe only two or three will become managers. The rest of them will go out, and when they go out what happens? Five years down the line the guy who stayed in and became a manager will be driving a nice car, staying in a nice house, and the other guy who quit will meet you on the way carrying CV's looking for jobs and begging for a taxi fare.

When I started last year, there was this guy who was in my office. He was trained by the same guy who trained the assistant manager that I promoted in December. But, he left. Last month, however, he came back and cried and gave a very good excuse as to why he had gone and not come back. He then said he was now prepared to work harder. The assistant manager doesn't like it when he trains someone and that person becomes a manager and that lady is making a lot of money and she can save. I thought this guy was honest about wanting to come back and work and so I gave him the opportunity. On his very first day back we gave him merchandise, he went to the field and never came back: he ran away with the merchandise. He was actually working under the assistant manager, someone he himself had trained. That assistant manager took him out on re-train and he ran away with all the merchandise. But they see him in the location, he doesn't have cloths to wear, that's the kind of people you work with. So it's like they have this mentality of wanting to live for today, when they work, they work for today, they don't think about tomorrow. Generally, most African immigrants make more money than the average South African, not because they are sharper or more lucky, but because they stay focused on whatever they do with a progressive attitude and an ambitious mentality. Then when they establish businesses and create employment for South Africans, or go to school and obtain scarce skills and pick up good jobs, they get rewarded with xenophobic attacks and claims that they came to take their jobs and women. Which lady these days will not fall for a hardworking, progressive, ambitious and loving guy, no matter where he originates from? That's my observation of the South Africans I work with. By no means should this be generalised to all South Africans.

On the other hand, I've come across a couple of South Africans who are very xenophobic. A majority of the Black South Africans that I have worked with have the mentality that they must take from you because you are a foreigner. They think that you get to their country and make a lot of money and that you must give it back to them. I've got a message in my phone. This message has been there for about two to three years now. It is a message sent by one of the people one of my managers promoted. He was working in the Cape Town office. The manager that promoted him left the business. It's one of those things. Even managers leave. They will leave, go squander all the money that they made and come back. So this guy was making money, but always he would take from me in the form of a loan, he wants a loan, he wants help. And I used to give thinking that I was helping him out. But it was a big issue when I gave him a lot of money and then asked him to pay it back.

He was dismissed from the company by the boss in Durban because of his bad working habits. Apparently, he thought I was the one who caused his dismissal when he sent me this message using a different cell phone number: "Hey man, be careful, I know where you live in Goodwood. It's an easy territory. You forget what you did to my brother. I think December will be too far to pay for what you did. You must watch." He pretended that someone else had sent the message. And, frankly speaking, at this point I had become very scared because I had also received another one. The company was overhauling; it was during the period of recession and they dismissed many managers. But these guys thought that since I promoted them, I was the one, even if I was not the one, who had not defended them enough and had led to their dismissal.. But they didn't know that I was also going to leave.

So the mentality these guys had was that I was making money in South Africa. They saw me as making money in their offices. They saw this as unjust – that they had to work for me. In turn, they assumed I must share my money with them. But the system does not say that. The system says I should give them the same opportunity that was given to me, so that they can make the kind of money that I make. And I gave it to them. What did they do with it? They want me to share my own money with them. There is one of them in Johannesburg, Taylor, who was also a manager that I promoted. At one time I was going to Cameroon. I think it was when I lost my dad. He called me on the evening of the day I was to leave. The Cameroon tradition says when you lose someone your friends should contribute and help you out. Instead, he called me and said he had not paid his car instalment and that I should lend him R3,000. It was a do or die situation, if I don't give him the money, he will lose his car. I transferred the R3,000 to his account, then I went to Cameroon. When I asked him for that money back, it became a war. He got so irritated and said, why do you ask me for R3,000? This is money you made in my office; I've been working for you. You are foreigners and you come and make money here. But this is money that he pleaded and I gave him to pay for his car instalment. People like that, they never make it in life. He was dismissed from the company. He is nothing now. The same as the car he lost after paying for so many years. You lend them money all the time, then most of them never pay you back, they forget, and just come back for more.

The first person who trained me when I joined DS Max in Cape Town consequently became a manager. He has been prostituting from one company to another and from one division to another and he is nothing today. In the other company we worked with he was actually a vice president. A vice president is a big, big post. Racha was the co-vice president with Kuze and he was making a lot of money, a lot. They lived the good life. On the other hand, Kuze is making money as always. I don't know if he now saves and invests his money. But the last time I saw him he was running a successful business of his own in Cape Town. This is probably because he is not South African by birth. Today Racha doesn't even have a car or a house. He left that company and went to another one, then went to another one again, and keeps moving like that. He is indeed a loser who cannot find satisfaction anywhere. I am yet to see a South African, Black or Coloured, in my industry that has made it and who has protected his success. They always succeed, but they fail again. So that goes to prove the fact that they only make money for today. When they make money, they're excited and spend the money and when the going is tough, they chicken out, that is the way I see them.

They are so proud and they feel that because you are foreigner in post-apartheid Mandela Country, you can't tell them anything. They know more than you do. They always end up like that. I don't know why, but when I work with South Africans now I so knowing full well that they can leave at any time. I make sure I don't make myself too good a friend with them, much as I would most dearly like to. The one who was sending me the threatening message is doing so probably because we were friends and he used to come and go to my place as it pleased him. He knows my home. This time, I don't take them to my house. They don't know where I stay. They don't know anything about me, we work in the office and that's it. But God knows how much I would really love to be warmer and brotherly with them.

Chapter 11

My Mother Was a Very Good Friend

When I think about my mum, I consider her one of the most exciting influences in my life. My mother was my mother, but she was also my friend, a very good friend. I could discuss anything with my mother, stuff that I could not so easily discuss with my father. My mother was a very good listener. She used to love me for who I was. She was the kind of a woman who would encourage you to do what your mind told you to do. She would just let you go about your business, but at the same time, she gave you direction here and there. I really loved my mum.

I had problems with my father. I never spoke with my father in a normal way. In one instance my father didn't communicate with me for about two years because I made up my mind that I was going to marry from outside the village. My dad was the kind of dictator who said it is either his way or the highway.

The only person I found encouragement and love in during that time was my mother. She was the first person in my family to say if you love that woman the way I see it, go for it. She was the only one who understood and supported me. That was the kind of person that she was. She would love you, support you for the kind of person you are, and she would also advise and encourage you. My grandfather only accepted it because of the trick my cousin and I played on him. But my father, until he saw my kids, his grandchildren, he was not in favour of the relationship. He loved grandkids so much, Penn and Muluh, especially when I took them to visit and spend the holiday with him in Payak City. That was shortly before he passed on. He died a fulfilled man.

I really regret that my mother passed away when I was not able to support her, pay her back for all what she did for me. It really made me feel bad. When I think of it now, if my mother was alive today, she would be a very big part of my life, even though I am here in South Africa. She would have been here with me, babysitting the kids and giving direction to my life and to the lives of those around me. When I used to leave my mother and stay away, even for a short while, I felt something was missing. That's how close we were. I was the first born and whatever I do today, I owe it to what I grew up doing at home. I was the only child for some time and I was the only support that my mum had for some time and most of the things that mothers need you to do are things that are, today, done by women. I became very useful at home. I took care of my junior ones. I cooked for them. I washed their clothes. I did almost everything a mother would do when she was absent. She taught me all that. And back home in a traditional society there are farms on which subsistence and survival depend.

My mother used to farm. The one farm was basically for cocoyams, the other one for maize and a few additional items. Back home the norm was that subsistence farming was for women, not for men, but because I was the first born, my mother taught me how to farm. I could go and clear the farm, clear the grass, mould ridges, plant corn, harvest, and I could do all of those things. That's what my mother taught me to do. She didn't look at me as a man. I don't know the way she looked at me because everything that a woman could do she taught me how to do it.

My mother came from the same village as my father but my maternal grandma came from outside Pinyin. I also grew up with my maternal grandmother for some time. I was also attached to her during my childhood. She came from Akum.

She was a princess from the Akum palace. So my mother also grew up there in Akum. Akum and Pinyin are geographically not that far apart. They are more or less the same people. There is not much of a difference in culture. We talk and understand each other. I might not be able to speak Akum fluently but I understand it. I'm not good with learning new languages. When I meet my aunties from Akum they speak Akum and I speak Pinyin and we both understand each other.

My mother was not the only wife that my father had. My father got married to his second wife when I was in class seven in primary school. She's still alive today. It was when I was in university that my father met his second wife. She stands out in my mind because I was still at home and it was very exciting to have another mother. In those days it wasn't like today where women don't like other women to come and share with them. It was the first wife who looked for the second wife, so it was my mother who found my father's second wife. My mother and the second wife were related, remotely. She had virtually looked for her sister to come and help her.

I grew up to meet the family like that. I grew up to like my step brothers and step sisters, and to respect my step mother. My family was very close. In my family when we grew up at the time, I had no place that I could call mine. It was a situation where my step mother was just like my mother. Most of the time it was my step mother, not even my mother, whom I visited first when I came back from school. It just happens that you associate more with the other women and we did things together. Even with my cousins we had such a family that wherever you went, you were welcomed.

I was born in Ngali, one of the quarters in Pinyin. That's where our big compound is. So when I was born my father then decided to move. It was my father and his junior brother and his step brother. They decided to move from Ngali to a new layout of their own. Presently, that's the place called Payak City. So they moved over there and the three brothers were in one place and it was like one family. Most of the time friends would not know whose father was whose. Most of the time friends didn't even know who your real mother is. When occasions arose and they needed your mother or father stepmothers or uncles would step in to speak as though you were their son. Our family is still very close, even though there are some cracks now with the growth. As I was growing up, however, I was in a close family. I spent my holidays in Ngali, for instance, in our big compound there, or at my uncle's place: not in our compound in Payak City

There are always certain bad things that you remember about people. It's normal. With all the good memories there's always one bad one that stands out. It is about an uncle of mine who was the government officer in charge of cleanliness in the village and its surroundings. I can't remember this incident enough.

He did something to me, and still, today, he can never be my friend. He has tried but we can never be friends. This incident is a block between us.. I always think about what he did. As I have related already, at one time my father was in prison, and I needed school fees of 300 francs. I went to this uncle and he told me he had no money but I knew that he had money. His own kids were going to school. He was my paternal uncle, my father's stepbrother, to be exact. If I went to him at that time, it was because I considered him my father. That's the way we were brought up, to see and relate to our uncles as our fathers. But how can I consider an uncle like this one a father when he refused to relate to me as his son? It takes two to tango. Being a father or a son is not merely a matter of birth or custom; it is a reality activated and kept alive by particular ways of relating to one another. A father who is there only in name is not worth having. The reverse is true; a son or child who is there only in name is equally not worth having. This consciousness might explain why the disappointment with my uncle over the school fees of 300 francs has stayed with me like a wound that refuses to heal.

At the time the other uncles who were down there in Payak City were not at home. My grandfather who was also my uncle was not at home. So the government officer was the only uncle that I thought could help me out. I went to him. He was educated. My father and his brothers had jointly sponsored him in school. He was the only person who went to school out of all my uncles. Well there was another one who died. I thought this uncle would understand that I am not going to school because of 300 francs. I went there and he gave me a lame excuse – he didn't have money. He didn't say please can you come back next week? He said he didn't have money. He didn't even say here is 100 francs, try and advance it, and come back later for the rest. No, he said he didn't have money. So those are some of the cracks by people like that, cracks that keep the family divided. Families are like every other institution. There are always some who don't fit in even when others are together. There are some who simply do not have the spirit of a family. We learn to live with that. Life must go on.

My mother was a Baptist Christian and I grew up to be Presbyterian, and eventually converted into Islam. Today I am back to practicing Christianity. My mother was Baptist because of where she came from, the majority of the people there were Baptist. So she grew up to be Baptist. When my parents married my father was not a Christian. At the time the church in Payak City was Presbyterian. My mother stayed Baptist, but allowed me to go to the Presbyterian Church in Payak City. My mother was that kind of person. She did not seek to impose her will on anyone. She said go to whatever church you want to go to. She was unlike a lot of parents in those days who used to influence the religion of their kids. Some of us, such as my junior brother, went with my mother to the Baptist Church because they liked it, not because they were forced.

I can't say for sure what accounts for my mother's open mindedness. I guess it was her nature and the nature of her family of birth. Maybe, it's inheritance because my grandmother came from Akum and got married to a Pinyin man. I guess that also influenced her reasoning. She was not thinking traditionally. She was not thinking like a normal Pinyin man or woman. She also grew up in Akum, so maybe those two traditions played a part in her open mindedness. Traditionally, my mother's family in Akum is very open-minded. I guess she got it from them.

If I am open-minded at all, I would credit it to my mother. My hustling nature is certainly from my father. My father was like that. As I have already indicated, my father used to go to Nigeria as a trader. He went to prison because he used to go to Nigeria to buy gun powder and matches. Even at that time, importing matches from Nigeria was illegal. He used to go and smuggle them into the country. He went to prison and while in prison he became a brick layer, a carpenter, he became everything and after he came out of prison, he built all the houses in our compound. He could build a house - from the foundation to the roof. All he needed was building material. That was my father. I'm not a handy man like him. But, as an adventurer, I would think that I am very much like him. I like taking risks, and I've come to believe that taking risks is the only thing that makes one grows. If you don't take risks you don't change or grow. My father was like that as well. It was a great risk to go to Nigeria on foot in those days. When he came back he was imprisoned, and when he came out of prison he didn't just fold his arms and say never again. He didn't say that since I went to prison I must go and stay at home. He started trading in cattle. He would go to Nkambe, buy cattle and take them to Kumba and sell them there.. So he was adventurous and it could only be someone who was willing to take risks to do the sort of things that he did in his life.

At one point, my father was a jack of all trades. He did almost everything. He actually trained me to hustle. He used to take me to Bali. We used to trek to Bali. It was quite a distance. We used to go to Bali and move from door to door buying coffee, and I had to transport that coffee on my head from Bali to Pinyin. It was a distance of about 40 km to 50 km long, and the roads were very bad. Maybe that's why I am what I am today. When I look at it, all of those things we used to do, it was just me who did this with my father. My juniors never did those things, what they did was very limited. I used to go with my father to Bali and buy coffee from door to door and even carry it back on my head and walk throughout the night to Pinyin, and we would take it to the farmers union to weigh the coffee and sell it. We used to go to Widikum and Ashong to buy and sell. We travelled a lot and that adventurous spirit paid off because in village terms my father could be considered rich. He could afford to send all his kids to school, pay our school fees, buy our books, and provide for us. I would say that the spirit of adventure, and taking risks could have come from my father.

I know I have already said this, but the fact is worth repeating: my father, in general, was a loving man. He loved his kids. I do understand. I told him so when I went to see him when he was sick two years before he died. I took my kids home, he was really sick and I took him to the hospital. He was in the hospital for quite a while, and he had started building a very big house in our compound when he fell sick and didn't complete it. I went and took him to a more efficient hospital, the Mbingo Baptist Hospital, where he was hospitalized. He didn't know that I had work going on in the compound. I fixed that house, completed it, painted it, and equipped it with modern furniture and things. So, on the day he was discharged, that was the day that the Pinyin people said my father died and I kept him in the mortuary and prepared for his funeral. That was the rumour from "radio one battery" – the gossip channel, as we would say back home. But it was my goal, I went home to execute that plan. When I got there, however, he was sick and I had to take him to the hospital. So they started saying that I was doing it because my father had died and I had kept him in the mortuary and I was preparing for the funeral before bring him home for burial. People started getting ready to eat. Funerals at home are eating and drinking opportunities. People warm up especially for the funeral of someone that they know has got money to spend, or someone whose child is a bushfaller – the term they use to refer to a Cameroonian living abroad.

When my father came out of the hospital I organized a dinner at home. I don't know what made me do it but I was so glad I had done it for him. It gave me a sense of fulfilment. I organized a very big ceremony at home, invited the whole family, the whole quarter and it was like a funeral as they wanted. I gave drinks, food, killed a cow, they cooked, it was so big. I guess I wanted to welcome my father from hospital and to celebrate his new house. But my father didn't know all that. I deliberately kept it as a surprise for him. So I took him from Abakwa and we drove to the village in the morning. People were just coming in. I drove right to the compound and my father came out and looked at the place. He was spellbound. He just stood there lost for words. He was probably wondering if it was his compound or if I had taken him to someone else's compound. I took him in. He just sat there. I could see the look of total bewilderment on his face. That was what gave me the satisfaction, the look on my father's face. It was also a look of thank you without saying so in words. He just looked appreciative and I was very happy that I made my father happy. That was the first time I saw my father lost for words. He couldn't say anything. So, during that ceremony, I told him all the bad things that he had done to me. I think I still have the CD recording somewhere. I told him all the bad things I could remember that he had done to me, especially the incident when I harvested pears from the compound and was given the thrashing of my life.

At the end, I told him, "Papa, I know everything you did was for my own good. I know you love me, and I really truly love you Dad." I know that all the things he did to me he had done because he loved me and he wanted me to grow up to be a good person. I don't think that I've disappointed him even if I've done a couple of things that he didn't like, like getting married to a woman out of the village. He didn't hate my wife. He liked her, but he hated the idea of me getting married to an outsider. As a matter of principle, he never wanted that, not for his first son. I told him the bad things he did to me and the only one thing that I could think of that my father did to me was that incident that I narrated. It was just that one. I would have called this a bad thing, the fact that I was still young when my father was in prison. I could still remember when my mother was working in the farm and I was on her back. I was very big at that time. My junior sister was born about four or five years after me, so I was a baby for a very long time.

I can't remember exactly for how long my father was in prison. Maybe two or three years. I can still remember my mother travelling with me on her back, working, and then my uncle who filled in. He was next door, he became a father. It means that I didn't see much of my father in the early years of my childhood life, I didn't see my father for three years, which for me I could have thought was something bad. But I don't think he was the cause, he was just trying to feign for the family. He was trying to make a living. So that's it. There's nothing much. When he refused to talk to me after I made up my mind that I was going to get married to this woman, we went for two years without talking to each other and I still passed the exam to go into the National College for the Training of Marines (NCTM). And my father was so proud of it. He became so excited about it that he forgot we were not talking to each other. So when I came home, I met him in the Ndapang market, he came and held me and was so pleased, "Well done my son, you made us proud." Unfortunately, however, I failed the oral part of the exams.

When I was going to the university, my parents said, "You've got a brother there. You've got your brother in the capital. He's a teacher in the university, so you cannot lack anything." That's what they said and I went there. This is the same person who, when we decided to go and write that exam, we went up to him, because we knew he was teaching at the national Marines college in addition to being a professor social psychology at the university. We went up to him and he said, "It is a good school, go and write." Maybe he was encouraging us knowing that we would never get that far. It was me and my cousin. Tennu was even closer to him than me. So he said he knows most of the people who are there. The exam was in four stages. There was the medical. If you pass the medicals, you go for the physical test. If you pass that one, you go for the written. After the written came the orals. And after the orals you could consider yourself admitted into the school. Success at each stage opened the way for the next stage, and failure meant elimination. We went to him to tell him because we knew that he could help, knowing Cameroon in those days.

He encouraged us. We went there for the medicals, both of us passed, passed the physicals, I used to train; I used to leave my quarter in Abakwa, Metta Quarter and run for miles to Akum and even as far as Santa and back. That's how good I was then. On the day of the physical, we had to run around the Ahmadou Ahidjo Stadium five times. I was first in my group, a group of about thirty people. That's how good I was in the physical. I passed that one and went for the written and passed. My cousin was successful as well, so we went and saw Dr Zunka, the well-placed brother in question, to remind him that we had succeeded and it was now time for the orals, where much did not depend on one's intellectual abilities, but rather on the subjective opinions of the members of the jury, and often on who could out-bribe whom. He was surprised that we had passed.

Dr Zunka pretended not to know that we had passed. So we asked him what next? The orals are coming up and he said, "It's fine, don't worry you'll pass." He was a member of the panel that asked us questions. I knew that even without his intervention I would pass. When I came out of the orals, I knew there was no way I could fail. The questions that I was asked were so straightforward and easy that I could not see myself failing the orals. Every member of the jury was nodding with every answer that I gave. Only Dr Zunka didn't ask me any questions. I left the place and I thought I had passed. But when the results came out I failed, both of us failed and we were the only two Pinyin boys who had passed everything up to the written part of the entrance examination.

I came to the conclusion that he didn't like to promote people from his area. In the village, many people have come to the conclusion that he wants to be alone. He wants to be the only eye, even to his own close family, that's what they think.

How bad can it get?

He would claim he sponsored his junior brother, although the brother has a different story. In the same way, he used to claim that he sponsored me. Some villagers believed he sponsored me until I told them that that was not true. His very own brothers know that he wants to be left alone, he wants to be the lone star. That's his character. When your father is alive and you want to *chopchair* you pretend to be good, you come to him and say nice things and do nice things, but you are just putting up a front. You want to pass for what you are not. It's like bribery. That is what he did before his father died, so he was anointed successor when clearly his character did not qualify him for such an honour. But because he was the rich man of the family, he was the educated one and he bribed his father, tried to pose as the good one.

I have a memory of my mother. The last time I saw my mother was in 1994, around March. I was to leave Cameroon. I went home and I knew that I was to say goodbye to my mother. I didn't want anyone to know that I was leaving the country. Not even my mum because I knew she would be worried if I told her the truth. So I still have this memory of her, that last time I saw her, when I went home that day. My stepmother was in the hospital, she was actually sick. I left home and my quarter is far from the hospital, so I had to walk with my mother. There was no taxi. I had to walk from our compound right up to the hospital and we spoke a lot. I remember that we were talking like mates, like friends, and my mother was going to the hospital to visit my stepmother. So we went there, visited her, and I told mama that I was going to the North for some business, that I might not see her for some time. It was okay. Now I knew in me that I was going out of the country and I didn't know when I would be going back, so when I was leaving my mum, I was almost crying, thinking, I will not see this woman for quite a while. She didn't know that. I left. The day that I left, we were in front of the hospital, and she stood waving at me, just waving and smiling when the taxi drove off, it's always in my mind. I left her there, waving at me with a smile, I could see her murmuring something like "good bye my son" as if she was saying her final good bye. I didn't know that that was going to be the last I saw of her. I only realised that when she actually died. I left in March and she died in June that same year. She was not actually sick. She went to my immediate junior sister, Manyi, who had just had a baby. She's married.

My mother went to the stream to wash clothes and fetch water, and she slipped and fell. The rainy season makes the ground slippery and she slipped and fell, and from there she died. She just died. That's what I heard. So she didn't die because she was old, she didn't die because she was sick, it was just an accident. But I didn't know that she died because at that time no one knew where I was and I was not communicating with anyone at home, so I only knew sixteen months after I left Cameroon and arrived in South Africa. Then I called, even when I called back home, they didn't tell me. I think I knew that my mother had died when it was twenty months or so. That is always on my mind: the last sight I have of my mother. She was there; she went to see my stepmother. She was standing in front of that hospital in Tisaghli, Pinyin, just waving, smiling and murmuring "good bye my son."

When I think of my mother, and the fact that Sma, my wife, is expecting a baby girl, I consider myself blessed. The doctor tells us to expect the baby early May. I have already named the unborn girl after my mother, Waah. I am also thinking of starting a project at home. Like a little thing in the memory of my mother. I intend to identify something she used to like. I am thinking of putting a little money aside to create a foundation in her honour and then promote a particular thing that she used to like. Moma, my kid brother, actually thinks we should sponsor a group of orphans, like us, especially those who have lost both parents, in school beginning from primary school right up to tertiary, on merit as they progress. This will start from Pinyin and expand to other villages as time goes on. So we have started with a few kids under the WAAP Foundation (Waah and Penn; Waah being our dear mum's name, and Penn our Dad's name.)

There's actually something that I've been doing. I know I actually inherited that from my mother, something that she would very much have wanted me to do, being generous. My mother was so generous. My mother would prefer to go hungry than to see you go hungry. She was that kind of person and I guess that's how I am too. I've been doing it a lot, helping people. My mother played a big part in my life. She was my friend, my guide and my inspiration.

She was a good woman, that's how I remember her. You never appreciate anything till you don't have it. When I was in Cameroon, I made some money but when I think of it now, what did I do with that money, what did I do for my mother? I didn't do anything, and she didn't mind. How I wished I had made her feel my gratitude in a special way when she was still alive!

She never minded. Those who really love you don't mind. It's those who don't love you who mind a lot. My mother was that kind of woman. You come like this and even if you brought a million and say mama, this is one million, she'll ask you, have you seen your auntie, have you seen your uncle, take, go and give to them. Her own riches were the relationships which she wanted to maintain and as long as you had good relationships with the people around her, she was fine. That's how some people are rich, rich in good relations, not material things. She was like that, she was not materialistic. She would never ask you for anything. Those that ask for things are those that do not care about you as much as – certainly not as much as my late mother cared for me.

With my father, I did the best I could. I did what I could afford to do while he was still alive. My only regret about my mother is that I never had the opportunity to give back to her what she gave to me.

Hopefully, the fact that I am giving to other people, including the people I used to house when I came to Cape Town, and including all those I have helped along the way, is a way of giving back to my mother. So, in a way, if she was still alive, that's exactly what she would be doing to people. I am to continue with what she used to do.

There's one thing though, that I still have to do. I know that she would have wanted me to do it as well. My uncle Ni, her junior brother, helped me a lot. He's now a retired soldier. I spoke to him not so long ago. When I was coming to South Africa, after I had lost everything at sea, it was his bakkie, his Hilux, an old Hilux that he revamped that kept me going. Actually, his brother owed him some money and couldn't pay him and gave him the bakkie. It was an old abandoned thing that my uncle used a lot of money to revamp. After bringing the bakkie back to life, he gave it to me. I was in Victoria at the time. I went to Abakwa and he gave it to me, because I told him I could use it to trade. I drove the bakkie down to Victoria and I made good use of it. I was selling *Fungeh*. I made quite some money with that bakkie, but I sold it when I was leaving because it was the only thing I had after running into unexpected difficulties.

Even though I've done so much for my uncle, he's retired and he continues to face financial difficulties. I send him money, and I sponsored his wife in school. His wife, Mami

Thesa, a personal friend who has been playing the role of mother to us for a long time, is so intelligent. But, she is someone who never got to see the four walls of a secondary school. Now, however, she's got the GCE Advance Level and she's got the Grade 1 Teacher's Certificate. She actually sat the A Level examination with Ron, her first child, the first time and passed while he failed. I sponsored her, paid her fees and many other things, and I am also sponsoring their first daughter in the University of Buea. Mama, she is a very clever girl, like her mother. I pay for her tuition and accommodation, and consider it my responsibility. But, I really wanted to do something bigger for him. I asked him, what must I do? I want to pay you back for that bakkie, and he said he doesn't want to hear about it. My house, the one house I bought in Abakwa, I gave him to control alongside the one bought by my kid brother, Moma. Although he has not exactly been responsible with the rents he collects, I am forgiving towards him. I know times are hard with him. I only learnt recently that he has not yet received the pension due to him by the government. It is already many years after his retirement. I will not blame him for not using the money the way I instruct him to. He has more responsibilities in the family than he can cope with, especially after the death of his elder brother, my uncle, and having to look after his three wives and many young kids. Although he is already getting a lot from me, here and there, I am still committed to doing something special for him because I promised myself that I would.

I think he's been retired for more than twenty years now. When he got married he didn't have a kid immediately. His kids came much later when he was approaching retirement, which means that he no longer had the energies to bring them up and sponsor them at school the way he would have done had he had them when he was young.

I had promised him that I was going to take his first kid, Ron, to South Africa and send him to school. But first I had to bring my first son, Taanji, and my other two kid brothers from Cameroon to South Africa. It would have been too expensive for me to bring all of them at the same time. As age mates with Taanji, the two of them were in the same school and class in Cameroon, and growing up together. So I asked my uncle's son to go on and do his GCE Advance Level in Cameroon, and I would bring him to South Africa after that. He was a very intelligent boy. I think he had eight or nine Ordinary level papers. But he went to high school and became something else. He did not study hard and did not have the advance level papers though, and he has, instead, joined bad company. So, I now refuse to honour my commitment. I am not going to bring someone to South Africa who is going to be a liability to me here. I am not interested in creating problems for myself. I already created enough problems bringing the two kid brothers to Cape Town who turned out to be as reckless and delinquent as they were back home. So I refuse. I have told my uncle that if Ron doesn't have his advance levels there's nothing that I can do. I don't want to associate myself with failures and delinquents. Ron actually disappointed me and his parents.

Last year Ron's kid brother passed his advance levels. So I am actually busy trying to get a visa to bring Ken here instead. That's something I wish to do in the next month. I already told my uncle to save some money from the rent of the house to help in this respect. I don't want him to continue to render the money invisible on unimportant family issues. Part of what he has saved will be used to sponsor the girl who is also at the University of Buea. I am doing everything to bring the boy here to go to university. I'm sure my mum would have loved for me to do that for her brother's son. She used to smile her appreciation when someone helped her brother and his family.

Currently, with my uncle retired, it's only his wife who is working with a private school. The school doesn't pay well. In fact, it pays very poorly.

I always think about paying back whatever good someone did for me, that is always in my mind, even if not directly to the person in question. Take the man who accommodated us in Zaire in Kinshasa for one year. I tried my best to find him. I always wanted to pay back the goodwill he had shown us through his unfathomable generosity. Unfortunately, I can't reach him in Zaire. So, instead, I try to do to others the good deeds he did to me and my friend when we were stranded. As for Judy, the one thing that has actually hindered me from looking for her with intensity is I know that she's married to someone. I don't want to resurrect our relationship at the level of intensity that might threaten her marriage. We've moved on with our lives. I don't want to expose skeletons in the cupboard. I have moved on with my life and she with hers. I don't want that kind of situation where our relationships will suffer. I know she's still out there and I know if there was a way that I could pay her back in person I would certainly do that. But I also want to respect her privacy; I also want to respect her relationship and not cause any problems for her. Actually I want her to be happy.

I am married to a South African, and I am happy. Sma is not Cameroonian, but she's wonderful. My parents just imagined that they refused me from getting married to someone who was from Cameroon, from the North West Province, from Abakwa, like me, because she was not Pinyin. Now, it's a South African that I am married to. I fail to understand the reason behind certain things. There are certainly advantages in marrying someone with whom you have a culture and close proximity in common. If I were married to somebody from my village, we would speak the same language, share a common history, know each other's families, and be able to relate to people without always having to second guess what they say or do. It's good. But, if you cannot find someone like that whom you love from your same culture, but you have someone else from another culture and another place that you love, why not go for her? I've taken Sma to the village. She's a dynamic woman. Everyone likes her, including my late grandfather. My father never met her before he died. I have three boys from my ex-wife, and Sma and I will be having a baby girl shortly. She's six months pregnant now, so very soon we'll be having a baby girl. Then at least we'll have one girl in the house, to give the boys a sister, so they will not think they are missing out on a sister.

My mind has always been set on returning to Cameroon to settle. When I left Cameroon at one point in time, my brother-in-law, my ex-wife's senior brother, Brother, as we all fondly call him, told me something that is with me at all times. He said something like, "remember that the moment you set foot on foreign soil it is at that moment that you start planning how to come back home," wise words, very wise words in deed. I've lived with that for nearly twenty years in South Africa. This urge to return back home has been fuelled by a couple of other people very close to me. My very dear sister, Fri, is one of them. I call her sister because that is what she is to me, a very true sister, though not biologically my mother's daughter. Fri is a legal luminary, a very successful lawyer in the South West Region of Cameroon who studied in the Nigerian Law School after her law degree in Yaoundé. Later on, while practicing law, she went to study for her LLM in the USA and is very active today in many legal organizations around the world. She is like me in many ways than one, a fighter, always dreaming big dreams and never relenting in her quest to add value to people's lives in any way she could. She, more than anyone else, has encouraged and assisted me to invest in Cameroon, especially in landed properties. She always visits me in Cape Town on holidays, sometime with her quiet but caring husband. Even over the phone and social media, she will always compel me to make the move, to start my journey back home. The other person who has been on my case to return home is my eminent cousin, Man Of The People. His name says it all. He is truly a man of the people; he is the one who conceived and launched the Pinyin Electrification Project. Thanks to him, we have electricity in Payak City and the rest of Pinyin. He is a philanthropist of the first degree. Some of my investments in Abakwa and Pinyin are thanks to this selfless individual. He would call me and encourage me to invest back home and to return back home.

In life, sometimes, most of the people who really care about you, who truly have your interests at heart and help you without expecting anything in return are not your blood relations. These are the people who will go out of their way to defend your interests, to help you. I want to go back home. I would not want the things I do in South Africa to jeopardise my chances of going back to Cameroon. I want to go back. When I started investing, I went to Cameroon. That was in 2005. At the time I was making money. I thought to myself I could actually go back to Cameroon every three years or so and buy a property. I decided that I was going to do just that until the point where I will have properties that will give me about the equivalence of my present earnings a month. Then I can retire back home. That was my goal. That was my dream.

That was basically the plan when I bought my first house in 2005. I came back to South Africa with that plan in my mind. I also encouraged my junior brother to go and buy a house. He bought one. I always try to encourage Moma and others who would listen to invest their money in landed property. Our dad encouraged us to do that too. But these plans are easier to make in abstraction. The idea of buying houses is a good one, but I have concluded that it would have to wait for when I am back to run things myself for the full returns of these investments to be realized.

I developed another plan to invest in South Africa instead. Buying property in South Africa where I could run things in person was likely to yield better returns than banking on investments that you cannot control. I realized no one can manage your business or investments the same way you can. Not in the way you would want it to be done. In addition, unlike Cameroon where it is cash or nothing, in South Africa, there is the facility of buying by bond. Another advantage of buying in South Africa is the ease with which one can resell. If I decide to go back to Cameroon today, I can sell all my properties in record time. When I buy property, I improve on it to add value, so that even if I sell today I will have a profit. With that profit I can take the cash along and invest it in Cameroon, knowing that I will be there in person to control the proceeds of my investments. My target was actually to go back in 2015. If I overstay that date, it should not be for too long. I have been negatively affected by having to change my business and also by the recession, but I believe I am still on target for 2015. I don't want to spend my 55th birthday in another person's country.

I know it will not be easy moving back permanently given my investments in South Africa and the fact that I have teenage kids that would better study in South Africa. But I do not have to sever links in a manner as if South Africa was never part of my life. I intend to be permanently settled in Cameroon before I get to age 55, but that should not be taken to mean that I intend to divorce South Africa.

As to why I want to return home, home is home. I feel that

my life won't be complete until I return to my roots. I am the *chopchair* or family head, and need to be at home to look after the family. I was not there after my father passed away – that affects me. A lot has gone wrong in the family. I also feel I can bring positive change to my people at large given the experiences I have had all these years. I have community projects I always wanted to execute but couldn't because of distance. I was born in Pinyin. I feel I must retire back there. The South African economy in recent times isn't helping either. It seems growth is really slow. The opportunities available to the likes of me when I first got here are fast drying up. The proliferation of shopping malls and corporate service providers means increasingly there is less and less relevance for the sort of things we have schooled ourselves to excel in. On the other hand, Cameroon, in spite of the bad business environment, is growing economically with more business opportunities for the discerning investor.

However much I aim to retire to Cameroon, South Africa will always be home as well. Through Sma, my wife, I have made a lot of South African friends that are still friends now. I am married to her family. It's like my family, and I've never seen a woman as modern as my present wife. Her family is one family where this thing they call xenophobia doesn't exist. They don't even think about it. This thing they call tribalism, of which my late father was very guilty when it came to choosing a girl for marriage, they don't even relate to it. It's a family that is very open. I would say I was lucky to have got a wife from that family. So I am very close to that family. How can one sever links from a people so reassuring, so human?

Sma's family is a very small family based in the Free State. Some of them are scattered all over. The immediate junior sister, Sibongile, is married in the Johannesburg area to Pule, a friendly and caring technician and both working for Sasol, an oil company. The other sister, Zanele, was studying at Vaal Technikon, but now on internship with a construction company in Port Elizabeth and always talking with playful seriousness about making Cameroon a second home in future. Why should anyone find that surprising?

None of them except my South African wife has been to Cameroon yet, but the future is full of promise. Sma has been to Cameroon two times. We will go again, maybe after she has the baby. We will have to take the baby to Cameroon. Sma has very good language skills. She visited Cameroon once, and has learnt to speak pidgin from her interactions with Cameroonians here in Cape Town. Her pidgin is as good as that of a native Cameroonian, born and bred. She just polished her pidgin up for the short time that we were in Cameroon. We were in Cameroon for six weeks, but even before she went there she was speaking pidgin. She's just sharp. She's good with languages unlike me. And when you have a heart for something you do it. She wanted to learn it. Her next target is Pinyin. As she opens up to the Pinyin and Cameroonian community, so they are opening up to her in equal measure. She is well and truly at home with and among them. Through my wife, I've come across a number of South Africans. There's one friend, Liburu, whom I knew through my wife's best friend, Tino. We keep in touch even now that he has moved to Johannesburg. We talk every now and then and he even visited from Johannesburg. He's such a great guy and I encouraged him to buy his first property in Summer Greens, in Cape Town. Apparently they, Tino and Liburu, studied almost the same thing in school. Liburu is like a brother to us. He just got married. Sma represented us at the wedding as I couldn't go for business reasons. They bought another property in the Kempton Park area in Johannesburg where they live now. There is also our sweet friend, Tino, Sma's childhood friend.

She was in Pretoria, she also went to the Technikon, was working with Telkom in Pretoria, and we used to visit her there. She asked to be transferred to Cape Town, to be close to us, so she was posted to Cape Town where she worked with Liburu in Telkom for about three years. Workers always change. They look for greener pastures. So just two years ago she got another job with Vodacom in Midrand, and she moved back to Johannesburg. She too bought her own property where she lives presently. She would come, even from Johannesburg, she would come spend a week with us, and we'd go visit her. There are other friends, a lot of South African friends, most of them through my wife, but none is as close as Tino. She would cherish a Cameroonian husband. She jokes about it, but I know she is serious. Their other childhood friend, Pinky, is married to a Cameroonian, Abdul, and they visited Cameroon last year. Those are about the closest South African friends that I've got. There's another one in Durban. She came to visit us here for a week and she's waiting for us to pay back. She's been bothering us to come to Durban, but busy-ness here cannot allow us. Perhaps they will visit us again before we visit them. Whenever I visit Cameroon, I bring back presents of various kinds (food, fabric, artefacts, music, etc.) for Sma's family and for our mutual friends. That's my way of wetting their appetite for my country of birth.

    I am going to name our baby girl after my mother. Waah is my mother's name and I intend the baby to reincarnate my mother. If Sma does not come with me to Cameroon immediately when I retire there, Waah will have to go to primary school in Cape Town. Once her mother has rounded up her nursing degree, worked here for some time, and joined me in Cameroon where we plan to open a clinic for her to run in Abakwa, Waah will come along with her, whether or not she has finished primary school. I intend Waah to complete her primary school in Cape Town and proceed to secondary school education in Cameroon. Apart from the excellent quality of secondary and high school education in Cameroon, schooling in Cameroon will offer an opportunity for Waah to bond with family there. I don't want a situation where my daughter fails to take advantage of her Cameroonian and South African roots in equal measure.

I want my daughter and wife to get to know in depth the village of Pinyin and the wider context in which I grew up. This should broaden her horizons and perspectives so that, when she is ripe for university, she could come back to South Africa for higher education. I want her to grow up into a sweet-footed daughter of Cameroon and South Africa, and a perfect example of a child of many worlds. She should go and come across borders as she sees fit, in the tradition of her nimble-footed mother and father who refused to be defined and confined by others.

Both Sma and I originate from rural backgrounds in South Africa and Cameroon, but we have refused to be immobilised by our backgrounds. We met in Johannesburg and settled in Cape Town, and in Cameroon she has been to Pinyin and Abakwa and is comfortable with both. These are the realities we want our daughter to embrace and celebrate. We want her to grow up in Cameroon and South Africa, speaking multiple languages and being accustomed to appreciating people from different backgrounds, different social positions and different countries. She is our hope of a truly rainbow pan-African future for our children and grandchildren in this beautiful continent. I can't wait to hold her in my arms, look into her eyes and say proudly: "Mum, you are back, welcome back".

www.ingramcontent.com/pod-product-compliance
Lightning Source LLC
Chambersburg PA
CBHW051353290426
44108CB00015B/1996